DAILY SUMMER ACTIVITIES

BETWEEN GRADES 7 AND 8

Writing: Rachel Lynette
Content Editing: Jo Ellen Moore
Andrea Weiss
Wendy Zamora
Art Direction: Cheryl Puckett
Cover Design: Liliana Potigian
Illustration: Judith Soderquist Cummins
Greg Harris
Jim Palmer
Design/Production: Carolina Caird
Susan Lovell
John D. Williams

EMC 1068

Evan-Moor®
EDUCATIONAL PUBLISHERS
Helping Children Learn since 1979

Congratulations on your purchase of some of the finest teaching materials in the world.

Photocopying the pages in this book is permitted for <u>single-classroom use only.</u> Making photocopies for additional classes or schools is prohibited.

Contents

Skills	1	2	3	4	5	6	7	8	9	10
Reading Comprehension										
Nonfiction	●		●	●	●	●	●	●	●	●
Fiction		●	●	●	●	●	●	●	●	●
Main Idea and Details	●		●	●	●				●	
Inference		●		●	●	●		●	●	●
Compare/Contrast	●				●					
Make Connections	●		●	●	●	●	●	●		●
Visualization		●		●		●	●			
Sequencing	●						●	●	●	
Cause and Effect										●
Prediction						●			●	
Theme		●			●	●	●	●		
Character and Setting		●	●		●			●		●
Grammar/Usage/Mechanics										
Spelling	●	●	●	●	●	●	●	●	●	●
Abbreviation					●					
Capitalization	●	●	●	●	●	●	●	●	●	●
Punctuation	●	●	●	●	●	●	●	●	●	●
Possessives		●	●			●	●			●
Quotation Marks					●	●	●	●	●	
Singular/Plural		●				●	●	●		●
Subject/Verb Agreement	●	●		●		●	●	●		
Compound Sentences	●							●		
Syllabification		●								
Negatives/Double Negatives						●		●		●
Sentence/Fragment				●						
Parentheses							●			
Subject/Predicate	●	●								
Parts of Speech:										
nouns/proper nouns	●	●		●				●		●
verbs/verb phrases	●	●	●				●		●	
adjectives									●	
pronouns	●	●		●		●			●	●
adverbs									●	
prepositions			●						●	
conjunctions	●									
Vocabulary Development										
Precise Language						●				
Idioms								●		
Silent Letters				●						
Base Words									●	
Alliteration						●				

Skills	1	2	3	4	5	6	7	8	9	10
Vocabulary Development (continued)										
Prefixes		●							●	
Suffixes	●		●		●				●	
Homophones	●									
Homographs										●
Heteronyms				●						
Compound Words								●		●
Synonyms					●					
Antonyms			●							
Blended Words							●			
Math										
Addition		●			●			●		●
Subtraction		●		●	●			●		●
Multiplication		●		●	●		●	●	●	●
Division				●	●		●	●		●
Word Problems		●	●			●		●	●	●
Pre-Algebra					●					
Place Value					●					●
Greater Than/Less Than/Equal to									●	
Fractions			●	●	●	●	●			
Function Tables		●								
Using Graphs/Tables/Charts	●	●	●	●					●	
Exponents								●		
Probability								●		
Measurement:										
units of measurement	●	●	●	●		●	●		●	
linear				●						
area/perimeter			●			●				●
angles		●								
Decimals/Percents	●		●	●		●				●
Polygons						●				●
Range/Mean/Median/Mode							●			
Geography										
Physical Maps	●		●							
Political Maps		●		●	●		●	●	●	●
Cultural Maps								●		
Population Maps				●						
Product Maps						●				
Legends/Keys	●					●	●		●	
Compass Rose/Directions	●	●	●	●	●	●	●	●	●	●
Thinking Skills										
Riddles/Problem Solving	●	●	●	●	●	●	●	●	●	●

About This Book

What's in It

Ten Weekly Sections

Each of the 10 weekly sections contains half- and full-page activities in several subject areas, including math, geography, reading comprehension, spelling, grammar, vocabulary, and critical thinking. The practice sessions are short, giving your child a review of what was learned during the previous school year.

Each week, your child will complete the following:

Read It!	2 comprehension activities consisting of a fiction or nonfiction reading passage and 4 multiple-choice questions
Spell It	1 spelling activity practicing the week's 12 spelling words
Language Lines	2 language arts activities practicing a variety of grammar and usage skills
Write It Right	1 editing activity to correct errors in spelling, grammar, and punctuation
Vocabulary	1 activity for building vocabulary and practicing such skills as compound words, word parts, synonyms, and homographs
Math Time	3 math activities on skills including word problems, fractions, and measurements
Geography	1 map activity testing basic geography concepts
In My Own Words	2 creative-writing exercises
Mind Jigglers	1 critical-thinking activity
Weekly Record Form	a place to record the most memorable moment of the week, as well as a reading log for recording the number of minutes spent reading each day

© Evan-Moor Corp. • EMC 1068 • Daily Summer Activities

How to Use It

The short practice sessions in *Daily Summer Activities* act as a bridge between grades, preparing your child for the coming school year by keeping him or her fresh on the concepts and skills mastered this past year. After completing the book, your child will feel more confident as he or she progresses to the next grade. You can help by following the suggestions below to ensure your child's success.

Provide Time and Space

Make sure that your child has a quiet place for completing the activities. The practice session should be short and successful. Consider your child's personality and other activities as you decide how and where to schedule daily practice periods.

Provide Encouragement and Support

Your response is important to your child's feelings of success. Keep your remarks positive and recognize the effort your child has made. Correct mistakes together. Work toward independence, guiding practice when necessary.

Check In Each Week

Use the weekly record sheet to talk about the most memorable moments and learning experiences of the week and to discuss the literature your child is reading.

Be a Model Reader

The most important thing you can do is to make sure your child sees *you* reading. Read books, magazines, and newspapers. Visit libraries and bookstores. Point out interesting signs, maps, and advertisements wherever you go. Even though your child is an independent reader, you can still share the reading experience by discussing what you read every day.

Go on Learning Excursions

Learning takes place everywhere and through many kinds of experiences. Build learning power over the summer by:

➤ visiting local museums and historic sites. Use a guidebook or search online to find points of interest in your area. The Chamber of Commerce and AAA are good sources of information about local attractions.

➤ collecting art materials and working together to create a collage, mobile, or scrapbook.

➤ going to a play, concert, or other show at a local theater or performance center.

➤ creating a movie of your child's favorite story. Write a simple script, make basic costumes and props, and recruit friends and family members to be the actors. Practice until everyone is comfortable before shooting the video.

➤ planting a garden. If you are short on space, plant in containers.

Spell It
This list contains all of the weekly spelling words practiced in the book.

A
accessible
accomplish
adjustable
administrator
adventurous
agency
ambitious
anonymous
anxious
appearance
assignment
assistance
associate

B
beachcomber
believable
beneficial
bouquet
broccoli
bungalow
burrito

C
campaign
chandelier
choreographer
cinnamon
comedian
commercial
compatible
conductor
confidence
contagious
convertible
courageous
courteous
curious
cyclone

D
delicatessen
depression
difference
disastrous
discussion
distinction
downstream

E
eligible
emergency
especially
essential
exchangeable
experience
eyewitness

F
featherweight
ferocious
finale
flammable
futon

G
genetic
gorgeous
gourmet
gracious
granddaughter
guitar
gymnasium

H
handkerchief
headquarters
hippopotamus

I
ignorance
inconsolable
independence
innocence
intelligence
intermission
invincible

J
journalist

L
laughingstock
lawyer
librarian

M
magician
maintenance
manager
maneuverable
messenger
moisten
mortgage
muscle
mythology

N
negotiable

O
obnoxious
orthodontist
outrageous
overemphasize

P
pajamas
patience
performance
perseverance
physicist
pneumonia
possess

potential
precise
professor

R
responsible
rhinoceros

S
sauerkraut
scissors
spaghetti
straightforward
subtle
succeed
succumb
sufficient
summary
surgical
suspicious

T
thistle
thundershower
tomb
transitional

U
underpopulated

V
vaccinate

W
Wednesday
wheelbarrow

© Evan-Moor Corp. • EMC 1068 • Daily Summer Activities

WEEK 1

Check off each box as you complete the day's work.

☐ ALL WEEK

☐ MONDAY

☐ TUESDAY

☐ WEDNESDAY

☐ THURSDAY

☐ FRIDAY

Spelling Words

appearance

assistance

confidence

difference

experience

ignorance

independence

intelligence

maintenance

patience

performance

perseverance

Get Creative!

Draw what you think you'll look like in 10 years.

A Memorable Moment

What sticks in your mind about this week? Write about it.

_____

_____

_____

_____

_____

_____

Reading Record

	Book Title	Pages	Time
Monday	_____	_____	_____
Tuesday	_____	_____	_____
Wednesday	_____	_____	_____
Thursday	_____	_____	_____
Friday	_____	_____	_____

Describe a character you read about this week.

_____

_____

_____

_____

_____

Read the article. Then answer the questions.

The Lawn Chair Flyer

Larry Walters was a truck driver who always dreamed of flying. When he couldn't get into the U.S. Air Force, he came up with a new plan. One sunny day in July of 1982, Larry made history when he took flight in a homemade aircraft near Los Angeles, California.

Larry tied 45 weather balloons to a lawn chair and used helium tanks to fill the balloons. Sitting in his sturdy chair like the proud captain of a ship, he ordered his friends to cut the anchor rope. But instead of rising slowly to a height of 100 feet as he had expected, Larry's aircraft rushed skyward. It rose to over 16,000 feet in the air. The truck driver with no flight experience was suddenly in airplane territory—in a lawn chair.

Fortunately, Larry had brought along a pellet gun and a two-way radio. He used the radio to communicate with surprised emergency officials. He also shot a few balloons with the pellet gun to lower his aircraft. However, the lawn chair eventually drifted into some power lines, causing a power outage in the nearby city of Long Beach.

After his historic flight, Larry had to pay a fine to the Federal Aviation Administration (FAA) for flying an uncertified aircraft. He complained that the Wright brothers, inventors of the first airplane, had also flown uncertified aircrafts. Later, Larry said, "I fulfilled my dream. But I wouldn't do this again for anything."

. . . .

1. How was Larry's lawn chair aircraft similar to most aircraft?

   Ⓐ It was certified for flight.

   Ⓑ It was propelled by balloons.

   Ⓒ It rose to a high altitude.

   Ⓓ It was able to land safely.

2. How is Larry similar to the Wright brothers?

   Ⓐ Both he and the Wright brothers experimented with flight.

   Ⓑ Both he and the Wright brothers had problems with the FAA.

   Ⓒ Neither he nor the Wright brothers had successful flights.

   Ⓓ Neither he nor the Wright brothers are famous.

3. The author compares Larry to the proud captain of a ship because Larry _____.

   Ⓐ was proud of his job

   Ⓑ was proud of his lawn chair flyer

   Ⓒ was proud of his friends

   Ⓓ was proud of his radio

4. How was Larry's flight different than he expected?

   Ⓐ It was very expensive.

   Ⓑ He flew higher than he thought he would.

   Ⓒ The chair broke.

   Ⓓ The balloons popped when he shot them.

Write It Right

Rewrite each sentence, correcting the errors.

1. my nieghbor gived me to hommade chocolate chip cookeys

   _____

2. did you no that tommorow is my dads birth day.

   _____

3. my sister and me have a wite dog named skippy,

   _____

4. my Aunt open a antique shop on Liberty street last weak

   _____

MATH TIME

Solve the percentage problems.

1. What is 40% of each number?

   5 _____   80 _____

   95 _____   110 _____

2. What is 75% of each number?

   8 _____   24 _____

   68 _____   200 _____

3. What is 23% of each number?

   6 _____   123 _____

   35 _____   76 _____

4. What is 7% of each number?

   3 _____   177 _____

   65 _____   234 _____

SPELL IT

The suffixes **–ance** and **–ence** are easy to confuse because they sound alike and have the same meaning. Both suffixes mean "the act of" or "the state of being."

Complete each spelling word for the week, using either the *–ance* or *–ence* suffix.

1. perform _____

2. differ _____

3. independ _____

4. mainten _____

5. ignor _____

6. intellig _____

7. assist _____

8. persever _____

9. confid _____

10. experi _____

11. appear _____

12. pati _____

In My Own Words

What was the best gift you have ever received? Who gave it to you? Why was it so special?

LANGUAGE LINES

The **simple subject** of a sentence is the main noun or pronoun of the sentence.
The **simple predicate** of a sentence is the verb in the predicate of the sentence.

Write the simple subject and the simple predicate of each sentence.

1. Ripe, juicy strawberries are my favorite kind of fruit.

   _____   _____
   simple subject   **simple predicate**

2. The book The Adventures of Tom Sawyer was written by Mark Twain in 1876.

   _____   _____
   simple subject   **simple predicate**

3. Adam, who is now my best friend, moved into our neighborhood last year.

   _____   _____
   simple subject   **simple predicate**

4. One person in the audience coughed throughout the entire performance.

   _____   _____
   simple subject   **simple predicate**

5. In the Atlantic Ocean, hurricanes are most common between June and September.

   _____   _____
   simple subject   **simple predicate**

MATH TIME

Fill in the blank to complete each math sentence.

1. 4 yards = _____ feet

2. $25\frac{1}{3}$ yards = _____ feet

3. 24 feet = _____ inches

4. 17.5 feet = _____ inches

5. 21 feet = _____ yards

6. 33 feet = _____ yards

Read the article. Then answer the questions.

Digging into Custer's Last Stand

For over a century, people have imagined the Battle of the Little Bighorn on June 25, 1876, as the brave "last stand" of General George Custer and his 7th Cavalry soldiers. Greatly outnumbered by Sioux and Cheyenne warriors, Custer and all 210 of his men died.

The belief in Custer's bravery started because of how the battlefield looked when it was discovered. A cluster of bodies, including the body of Custer, was found along with dead horses on a hill. People wanted to believe that the soldiers put up a good fight. Some Native American accounts also described the soldiers' bravery. Over time, a story developed of the soldiers on the hill fighting heroically to the end.

Then, in 1983, a prairie fire swept through the battlefield in Montana. The blaze burned off grass and shrubs, making it easier to dig for bullets and gun cartridges from the battle. Archaeologists examined old evidence in a new way, using modern methods of investigation. These methods gave new clues about what had happened to Custer and his men.

Using the bullets they found, experts were able to trace the shots fired by both sides. This allowed the investigators to reconstruct the movements of different groups on the battlefield. Based on the numbers of certain bullets and where they were found, a different account of the battle emerged. Instead of fighting a long, brave battle, Custer's men may have panicked, become disorganized, and lost the battle in a short amount of time.

1. Information in the article _____.
   Ⓐ disproves the new theory of Custer's last stand
   Ⓑ raises doubts about the old theory of Custer's last stand
   Ⓒ questions whether Custer won the battle
   Ⓓ proves what happened to the horses

2. What first caused experts to reexamine what happened at Little Bighorn?
   Ⓐ new Native American accounts of the battle
   Ⓑ the discovery of the original battlefield
   Ⓒ new technology for studying bullets
   Ⓓ a prairie fire on the battlefield

3. According to the article, the newer theory about Custer's last stand started _____.
   Ⓐ just after the battle in 1876
   Ⓑ in the 1980s
   Ⓒ with the discovery of the soldiers' bodies
   Ⓓ with the belief that U.S. soldiers are always heroic

4. What did investigators do that supported a different theory of what happened at Little Bighorn?
   Ⓐ The investigators described eyewitness accounts.
   Ⓑ The investigators explained the methods of their investigation.
   Ⓒ The investigators proved why the soldiers died quickly.
   Ⓓ The investigators reconstructed movements on the battlefield.

Vo·cab·u·lar·y

Homophones are words that sound alike but have different spellings and different meanings. For example, **allowed** and **aloud** are homophones.

Allowed is the past tense of the verb **allow**, which means "to permit."
Aloud is an adverb that means "vocally" or "out loud."

A. Draw a straight line from each homophone to its definition or the picture that illustrates it. Each line will pass through one letter.

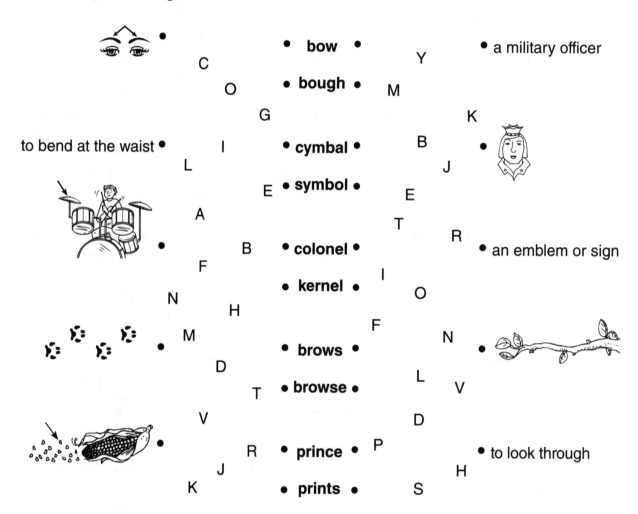

B. Unscramble the letters that the lines pass through on each side above to form another pair of homophones.

_____   _____

LANGUAGE LINES

Compound sentences are made by joining two or more simple sentences containing related information. They are formed using a comma and a **coordinating conjunction**.

Form a compound sentence by joining the simple sentences with a comma and the coordinating conjunction *or, and,* or *but.*

1. I looked for my homework on my desk. I forgot to look on the kitchen table.

_____

_____

2. Maybe I left it on the bus. Maybe I left it in the cafeteria.

_____

_____

3. I went into my bedroom. I found it under the bed.

_____

_____

In My Own Words

What has been the high point of your day so far? What has been the low point?

Mind Jigglers

Favorite Animals

Match each person with his or her favorite animal in the box. Read the clues in the chart to find the answers. Each animal may be used only once.

bear cub	chipmunk	hamster	monkey	puppy
calf	dolphin	kitten	mouse	rabbit
canary	fawn	ladybug	penguin	raccoon
chick	frog	lamb	piglet	squirrel

Name	Clue	Animal
Mara	is usually white	
Anthony	is a bird	
Fiona	lives in the jungle	
Laura	is an insect	
Daphne	has long ears	
Katie	contains four of the letters that are in her name	
Jake	lives in a cage	
Derek	was found at a pond	
Andy	ends with the same letter as his name	
Drew	begins with the same letter as his name	
Peter	contains the same number of letters as his name	
Lucy	is the third-smallest pet	
Shari	is a baby animal	
Annie	contains two pairs of double letters	
Kevin	is not a mammal	
Miranda	lives on a farm	
Chad	contains the same number of letters as his name	
Joey	stores nuts	
Luke	contains the same number of letters as his name	
Carl	begins with the same letter as his name	

MATH TIME

Plotting Coordinates

Plot the ordered pairs of numbers in the order in which they are listed. Then connect the points with straight lines. Start each new set of points with a new line.

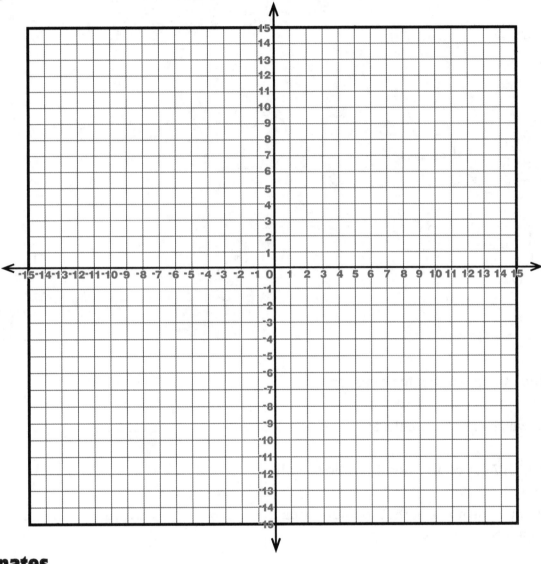

Coordinates

➤ **Set 1:** (–2, –10) (–1, –10) (–1, –9) (1, –9) (1, –10) (2, –10) (2, –7) (1, –7) (1, –8) (–1, –8) (–1, –7) (–2, –7) (–2, –10)

➤ **Set 2:** (7, –11) (7, –7) (6, –2) (5, 0) (4, –2) (3, –4) (1, –6) (–1, –6) (–3, –4) (–4, –2) (–5, 0) (–6, –2) (–7, –7) (–7, –11)

➤ **Set 3:** (–1, –4) (1, –4) (1, –2) (–1, –2) (–1, –4)

➤ **Set 4:** (2, 2) (2, 3) (4, 3) (4, 2) (2, 2)

➤ **Set 5:** (–2, 2) (–2, 3) (–4, 3) (–4, 2) (–2, 2)

➤ **Set 6:** (5, 0) (6, 6) (7, 2) (8, 1) (9, 1) (10, 2) (10, 7) (9, 9) (7, 10) (3, 11) (–3, 11) (–7, 10) (–9, 9) (–10, 7) (–10, 2) (–9, 1) (–8, 1) (–7, 2) (–6, 6) (–5, 0)

Geography

Australia and Oceania

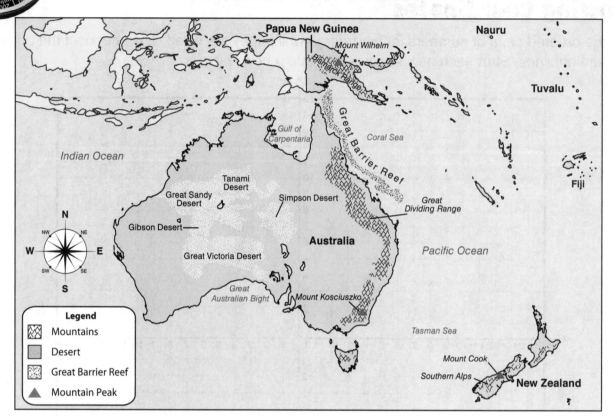

Use the map to answer the questions.

1. In which country are the Southern Alps located? _____

2. Which Australian desert is farthest south? _____

3. What is the name of the mountain peak in Papua New Guinea? _____

4. Which landform is located in the sea just off the northeastern coast of Australia? _____

5. Which Australian desert is farthest east? _____

6. What is the name of the mountain peak in Australia? _____

West of Greenwich   Longitude West of Greenwich

120°   B   150°   C   180°   D   150°   E   120°   F   90°

© Evan-Moor Corp. • EMC 1068 • Daily Summer Activities

WEEK 2

Check off each box as you complete the day's work.

☐ ALL WEEK

☐ MONDAY

☐ TUESDAY

☐ WEDNESDAY

☐ THURSDAY

☐ FRIDAY

Spelling Words

accomplish

associate

broccoli

commercial

flammable

hippopotamus

messenger

possess

scissors

succeed

summary

vaccinate

Get Creative!

Draw a creature that's a cross between a lizard and a zebra.

A Memorable Moment

What sticks in your mind about this week? Write about it.

_____

_____

_____

_____

_____

_____

Reading Record

	Book Title	Pages	Time
Monday			
Tuesday			
Wednesday			
Thursday			
Friday			

Describe a character you read about this week.

_____

_____

_____

_____

_____

_____

Read the story. Then answer the questions.

The Elephant and the Hummingbird

Long, long ago—in the days when people could talk to animals and learn their stories—an elephant walked slowly beside the Yellow River. This was before animals were tamed, even before the first Chinese emperors ruled. That's how long ago it was.

The elephant was enjoying a peaceful stroll. Thick grasses and beautiful lotus flowers bloomed, and the water in the Yellow River made a pleasant swishing sound as it flowed past the elephant.

Noticing what appeared to be a hummingbird, the elephant stopped. The elephant had seen hummingbirds before. He'd watched them hover above lotus flowers, their wings beating so quickly that they appeared only as a blur. The elephant sometimes wished he could move as quickly as a hummingbird. This one, however, was lying upside down, her wings motionless and her legs pointing toward the sky. Occasionally, the little bird would sigh heavily or grunt, as if working extra hard.

"What are you doing?" asked the elephant. He slowly walked around the hummingbird, trying to understand the odd behavior. "You look ridiculous, you know."

"I am holding up the sky," replied the hummingbird calmly. "I overheard that it might fall today."

The elephant raised his trunk and bellowed a deep, loud laugh. "You're holding up the sky? Why, just look at it. The sky is bigger than I am, and I doubt you could hold me up. Even if the sky were going to fall, your tiny legs could not possibly do the job."

"Ah," said the hummingbird, "but these are the only legs I have. I might not be able to do it by myself, but I am doing what I can."

. . . .

1. **Where and when does the folk tale take place?**

   Ⓐ on a ship on the Yellow River

   Ⓑ on a bridge around AD 1400

   Ⓒ in a Chinese flower garden

   Ⓓ beside a river in ancient China

2. **How does the elephant probably feel about what the hummingbird is doing?**

   Ⓐ He thinks she is smart.

   Ⓑ He thinks she is arrogant.

   Ⓒ He thinks she is wasting her time.

   Ⓓ He thinks she is selfish.

3. **What is the message of the folk tale?**

   Ⓐ People should do what they can with what they have.

   Ⓑ Past wisdom is better than present wisdom.

   Ⓒ It is always best not to look ridiculous.

   Ⓓ It is risky to try things that other people say are impossible.

4. **Which of these conflicts is important in the story?**

   Ⓐ good vs. evil

   Ⓑ trying vs. watching

   Ⓒ strength vs. weakness

   Ⓓ being tame vs. being free

Write It Right

Rewrite each sentence, correcting the errors.

1. only kids who has past the swimming test are aloud to swim in the deap end of the pool

   _____

   _____

2. at the zoo we, seen a lion a elefant and a giraffe,

   _____

   _____

3. maria always eat three shugar cookie's after dinner

   _____

MATH TIME

Complete the function tables using the given rule. The first entry has been done for you.

1.

Rule = × 3 – 12	
Input	Output
12	24
8	
	3
3	

2.

Rule = + 3 × 11	
Input	Output
2	
4	
9	
15	

3.

Rule = × 3 – 5	
Input	Output
19	
	40
8	
1	

4.

Rule = × 5 + 1	
Input	Output
	16
	21
	41
	51

Words are usually divided into syllables between double consonants, after a consonant that follows a short vowel, or after a long vowel.

lit|tle   pen|cil   pa|per

Write the spelling words for the week. Then draw lines to divide each word into syllables. Use a dictionary to help you.

1. _____

2. _____

3. _____

4. _____

5. _____

6. _____

7. _____

8. _____

9. _____

10. _____

11. _____

12. _____

In My Own Words

Your parents have decided that your new bedtime is 8:00 PM! What can you say to convince them that this is a bad idea?

LANGUAGE LINES

A **verb phrase** is made up of a **helping verb** and a **main verb**. Helping verbs include:
am   is   are   was   were   have   has   can   should   could   must   will

Write the helping verb and the main verb in the correct columns.

	Helping Verb	Main Verb

1. My town has built a new playing field. _____ _____

2. The football team can play on Friday nights now. _____ _____

3. You must come to our next game. _____ _____

4. We are improving every week. _____ _____

5. By the next game, we should be great! _____ _____

6. I know we will win our next game. _____ _____

MATH TIME

The Galloway family recorded the amount of money they collected at their garage sale in the chart below. Use the chart to answer the questions.

Person	Money Collected
Ginny	45¢, $1.75, 75¢, $1.25
Justin	$2.00, $2.00, $1.50, 25¢
Lucas	$3.00, $1.75, 30¢
Lia	90¢, 35¢, 25¢, 10¢, 75¢

1. How much money did each family member make at the yard sale?

Ginny: _____   Lucas: _____

Justin: _____   Lia: _____

2. How much money did the family make altogether? _____

Read the story. Then answer the questions.

Up to the Mountaintop

I like challenges, but this one was almost too difficult. I had begged Mom to take me on a completely new adventure for my sixteenth birthday. Now, here we were, just Mom and me with our guide, Milo, standing on the shore of Lake Arenal in Costa Rica. Towering above the lake was Volcán Arenal, one of the active volcanoes in the region. I watched as the volcano spit out lava and coughed up big boulders. Luckily, we were headed in the other direction.

Milo helped us mount our horses. Getting on my horse was difficult, but controlling it was a little easier. We started on our ride. The guidebook said we'd cross three rivers. As we splashed through a gentle stream, I asked hopefully, "Is this the first river?"

"I don't think so, Katie," Mom said wryly.

Soon enough, we came to a *real* river. There was no mistaking it. I felt sick to my stomach when I saw that the far shore was half a football field away! The four-foot-deep river flowed over large boulders. So much for dry shoes—or jeans.

After two more rivers, the trail got steeper and muddier. With each step of the horses' hooves, there were loud squishing and sucking sounds. The rainforest was magnificent and absolutely beautiful. But I wondered whether my horse could keep its balance in knee-high mud. What did I know about horses? I imagined my mare stumbling on rocks hidden beneath the sludge—and us crashing over a cliff and being swept away by lava.

Three treacherous hours later, we came to a corral. I wondered why we were stopping. To one side was a gorgeous view of the lake and volcano, and to the other, a brightly painted restaurant. "Okay," I laughed nervously. "That was scary, but I'm so glad we did it!"

. . . .

1. **Which adjectives best describe Katie?**

   Ⓐ sensitive and shy

   Ⓑ calm and relaxed

   Ⓒ adventurous but nervous

   Ⓓ interested but withdrawn

2. **Which inference can you make about Katie's experience riding horses?**

   Ⓐ She is an expert rider.

   Ⓑ She has probably trained others to ride.

   Ⓒ She dislikes horses.

   Ⓓ She has little experience riding horses.

3. **Which best describes the setting of the story?**

   Ⓐ dangerous

   Ⓑ boring

   Ⓒ busy

   Ⓓ crowded

4. **What is the theme of Katie's story?**

   Ⓐ What is familiar is better than what is unknown.

   Ⓑ Most people fail when they try new things.

   Ⓒ Fear stops people from trying new things.

   Ⓓ It is good to push yourself to try new things.

Vo·cab·u·lar·y

A **prefix** is a word part that comes at the beginning of a word and affects its meaning. Knowing the meanings of prefixes can sometimes help you figure out the meanings of words.

The prefixes **mega–**, **magni–**, and **macro–** mean "large" or "great."

The prefixes **micro–** and **mini–** mean "small."

Write *mega–*, *magni–*, *macro–*, *micro–*, or *mini–* to form words that will make sense in each sentence below. Then write the words to complete the sentences.

_____fy   _____tude   _____biotic   _____mum   _____ature

_____lith   _____cosm   _____phone   _____phone   _____scope

1. Coach Flexman uses a _____ to project his voice across the field.

2. Ancient people moved the giant _____ without machines.

3. I saw tiny hairs on the fly's legs when I looked at it under a _____.

4. The optometrist uses a lens to _____ images to 10 times their size.

5. Nick thinks a _____ diet will help him live to be 100 years old.

6. I love astronomy, so I want to study the entire _____.

7. The Richter scale is used to measure the _____ of earthquakes.

8. In order to amplify her voice, the jazz singer needed a _____ .

9. We bought _____ furniture for my sister's dollhouse.

10. The _____ speed limit on the interstate is 45 miles per hour.

© Evan-Moor Corp. • EMC 1068 • Daily Summer Activities

LANGUAGE LINES

A **compound subject** contains two or more simple subjects that are joined by a coordinating conjunction and share the same verb. A **compound predicate** tells two or more things about the same subject, without repeating the subject.

Write *compound subject* or *compound predicate* after each sentence. The first one has been done for you.

1. I did my math homework and wrote my essay.   <u>compound predicate</u>

2. Wendy lives in Holland and speaks Dutch.   _____

3. Carrie, Emily, and Jack went to the movies.   _____

4. Andrew ate a hot dog and scarfed down a hamburger.   _____

5. Mr. and Mrs. Benefit announced their new baby boy.   _____

6. Meghan watched her dog take off and chased after him.   _____

In My Own Words

Imagine you are a novelist working on your next mystery. Describe your main character. What is his or her name? What does he or she look like? Name at least two personality traits of your character.

Mind Jigglers

Clocks and Calendars

A. Complete the time-related phrases.
Example: 12 m<u>onths</u> in a y<u>ear</u>

60 s_____ in a m_____

100 y_____ in a c_____

24 h_____ in a d_____

52 w_____ in a y_____

60 m_____ in an h_____

365 d_____ in a y_____

31 d_____ in a m_____

10 y_____ in a d_____

72 h_____ in 3 d_____

120 m_____ in 2 h_____

24 m_____ in 2 y_____

B. Solve the time-related riddles.

Carrie practices piano from 3:10 until 3:55 PM. How long does she practice?

_____ minutes

Miranda babysat her brother for 3 hours and 45 minutes. She started at 11:30 AM. At what time did she finish?

_____

It took Samantha 47 minutes to do her homework. She finished at 8:22 PM. When did she start?

_____

Charlotte dances ballet for 2.5 hours twice each week. How many hours will she have danced in 12 weeks?

_____ hours

C. Guess the phrase. Look at the way the words are written, including word order and placement, to find the answer.

TimeTime

_____
_____

DAY'S all WORK

_____
_____

**S
E
M
I
T**

_____
_____

Geography

Canada and Greenland

The country of Canada is divided into ten provinces and three territories.
The territories are in the north, and the provinces are in the south.

Use the map to match the locations on the right to the clues on the left.

_____ 1. province east of Alberta and west of Manitoba   **a.** Yukon Territory

_____ 2. province bordering Hudson Bay to the east   **b.** Greenland

_____ 3. territory that is farthest northwest   **c.** Ottawa

_____ 4. ocean bordering Canada to the east   **d.** Québec

_____ 5. national capital of Canada   **e.** Nunavut

_____ 6. island north of Baffin Island   **f.** Saskatchewan

_____ 7. ocean west of British Columbia   **g.** Atlantic Ocean

_____ 8. territory bordered to the south by Manitoba   **h.** Pacific Ocean

Measuring Angles

Measure each of the angles in the orange box with a protractor (to the nearest 5°). Then write the corresponding letter above the angle measurement below the box. The letters will spell out the answer to the riddle.

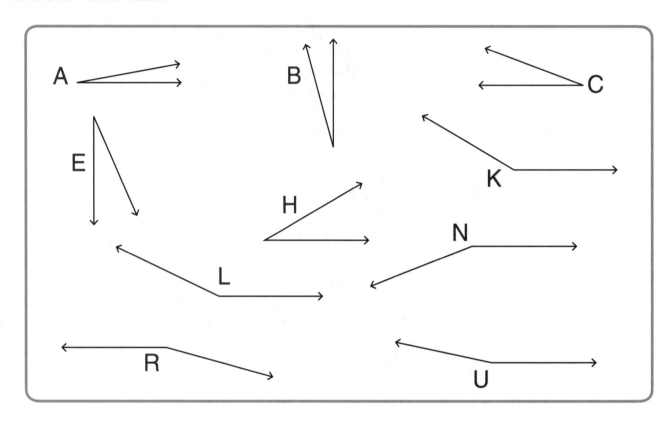

What is smashing and comes between morning and afternoon?

——— ——— ——— ——— ——— ———
10°   155°   170°   160°   20°   30°

——— ——— ——— ——— ———
15°   165°   25°   10°   150°

WEEK 3

Check off each box as you complete the day's work.

Spelling Words

adventurous

ambitious

anonymous

courageous

courteous

curious

disastrous

ferocious

gorgeous

gracious

outrageous

suspicious

Get Creative!

Turn this number into a picture.

2

 **A Memorable Moment**

What sticks in your mind about this week? Write about it.

_____

_____

_____

_____

_____

_____

Reading Record

	Book Title	Pages	Time
Monday	_____	_____	_____
Tuesday	_____	_____	_____
Wednesday	_____	_____	_____
Thursday	_____	_____	_____
Friday	_____	_____	_____

Describe a character you read about this week.

_____

_____

_____

_____

_____

Read the article. Then answer the questions.

Tall Tale Heroes

Life for American pioneers was hard, and their work was often tedious. For entertainment, they told funny stories called "tall tales." The stories had larger-than-life characters and were filled with exaggerations. Two famous tall tale characters are Paul Bunyan and Pecos Bill.

Imagine a giant lumberjack who could topple an acre of trees with one hand. That was Paul Bunyan. Bunyan was so big that he had to eat 40 bowls of porridge just to whet his appetite. His faithful companion was an immense blue ox named Babe. Their rain-filled footprints became the 10,000 lakes of Minnesota. According to stories, surviving in the North Woods was an achievement. One winter, it was so cold that Babe's milk turned straight to ice cream!

Do you know of any cowboy who would ride a horse named Widowmaker? That was Pecos Bill, who also galloped around on a mountain lion. Legend says that Bill fell from his parents' wagon when he was a baby. Coyotes rescued Bill and raised him in the wild. He could rope a whole herd of cattle at once, or even lasso a cyclone. And when he anticipated trouble, he carried a live rattlesnake as a whip. Bill's girlfriend was also famous for her frequent stunts. Sluefoot Sue once took a pleasant ride on a giant catfish down the Rio Grande River!

Paul Bunyan and Pecos Bill are just two examples of the imaginative characters who represented the hope and spirit of America's pioneers. Their stories still entertain us today.

. . . .

1. **A tall tale is filled with _____.**
   - Ⓐ historical events
   - Ⓑ mysteries and magic
   - Ⓒ exaggerations and humor
   - Ⓓ sad stories

2. **Which words describe Babe, the blue ox?**
   - Ⓐ slow, cranky
   - Ⓑ immense, faithful
   - Ⓒ tall, lazy
   - Ⓓ watchful, mean

3. **Who is *not* a character in a tall tale?**
   - Ⓐ Pecos Bill
   - Ⓑ Sluefoot Sue
   - Ⓒ Harry Potter
   - Ⓓ Paul Bunyan

4. **According to stories, one winter it was so cold that...**
   - Ⓐ birds flew backwards.
   - Ⓑ tulips bloomed in December.
   - Ⓒ hens laid hard-boiled eggs.
   - Ⓓ milk turned straight to ice cream.

Write It Right

Rewrite each sentence, correcting the errors.

1. woud you like too eat a apple or a bananna

   _____

   _____

2. in the united, states we celebrate independence day on july forth.

   _____

   _____

3. make shure that you dont let you're ice creem melt in the son

   _____

   _____

MATH TIME

Complete the table so that each row shows three representations of the same value.
The first row has been done for you.

Fraction	Decimal	Percent
$\frac{7}{10}$	0.7	70%
	0.3	
$\frac{3}{4}$		
		90%
	0.375	

SPELL IT

> The suffix **–ous** often means "full of."

Write the spelling words for the week to match the clues below. Then underline the suffix in each word.

1. full of a need to find out:

   _____

2. full of ambition:

   _____

3. causing outrage:

   _____

4. causing great damage:

   _____

5. full of beauty:

   _____

6. unidentified:

   _____

7. full of fierceness:

   _____

8. full of suspicion:

   _____

9. full of adventure:

   _____

10. full of courage:

    _____

11. full of grace:

    _____

12. full of politeness:

    _____

In My Own Words

Describe either the oldest or the youngest person you know. Include as many details as you can.

_____

_____

_____

_____

_____

_____

_____

_____

LANGUAGE LINES

A **preposition** shows the relationship of a noun or pronoun to another word in the sentence. Words such as **above**, **behind**, **during**, **with**, and **for** are examples of prepositions.

Circle the preposition or prepositions in each sentence.

1. Katie hid behind the big oak tree.

2. Tom fell asleep during the movie.

3. Sanjay made a birthday card for his sister.

4. James stretched his arms above his head.

5. Carlos looked in his pocket for his keys.

6. Tim eats his dinner with chopsticks.

7. Jen ran into a tree during a game of tag.

8. Maria went with her mother to the store.

9. Chris ran around the house in bare feet.

10. Ben crawled under the fence carefully.

MATH TIME

Solve the measurement problems below.

1. Find the perimeter of the football field in feet.   _____

2. Find the area of the football field in feet.   _____

3. How many feet away from the end zone is the 50-yard line?   _____

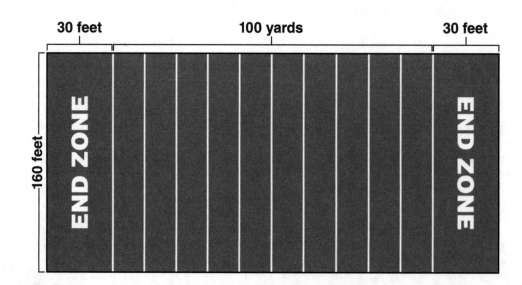

30 feet   100 yards   30 feet

160 feet

END ZONE   END ZONE

Read the story. Then answer the questions.

A Diagnosis

Every Sunday at exactly 11:00 AM, my whole family gathers in the lobby of the Oak Valley Manor for Senior Citizens. That's when my parents, my brother Phillip, and I join my great-grandmother June for Sunday brunch—a spectacular buffet of omelets, pancakes, and French toast. Great-Grandma June's friend, Dr. Shepard, always joins us.

Lately, though, there has been a change in Dr. Shepard, who also lives at the Manor. When I first met him, he used a walker to get around but still stood straight and tall and always smiled. Now he seemed to move more slowly, hunched over his walker, and rarely smiled.

Recently, our dog Sally had been tired and hadn't wanted to play. Since pets are allowed in the Manor on Sundays, we decided to bring Sally along. As we walked in, we heard Dr. Shepard holler, "Come, Sally!" He reached out his arms and Sally ran to him, her tail wagging wildly. He scratched behind Sally's ears and gently rubbed her belly.

"Dogs are wonderful!" he said. "And I should know. I used to be a vet."

"Wow, you were a vet? Maybe you can figure out what's wrong with Sally," I said.

Dr. Shepard chuckled. "Maybe I can!" And with a huge smile he added, "Go ahead and join your family. I'll stay right here with Sally and see if I can make a diagnosis."

· ·

1. **What change does the narrator notice about Dr. Shepard before Dr. Shepard sees Sally?**

   Ⓐ Dr. Shepard no longer joins the family for brunch.

   Ⓑ Dr. Shepard moves more slowly and smiles less often.

   Ⓒ Dr. Shepard is healthier and happier.

   Ⓓ Dr. Shepard is no longer friends with Great-Grandma June.

2. **What is the main idea of the passage?**

   Ⓐ A family brings their dog Sally to see a vet.

   Ⓑ The Manor has a great buffet every Sunday.

   Ⓒ Sally and Dr. Shepard are not feeling well but may be able to help each other.

   Ⓓ The family visits Great-Grandma June at Oak Valley Manor.

3. **Which detail from the passage tells you that something is wrong with Sally?**

   Ⓐ Sally is tired.

   Ⓑ Sally runs to Dr. Shepard.

   Ⓒ Sally wags her tail wildly.

   Ⓓ Sally visits the Manor.

4. **What does the family normally do at Oak Valley Manor?**

   Ⓐ They take Sally to see Dr. Shepard.

   Ⓑ They eat brunch with Great-Grandma June.

   Ⓒ They spend the morning with Sally.

   Ⓓ They pick up Great-Grandma June for a day out.

Vo·cab·u·lar·y

Antonyms are words that have opposite meanings.

Doubt is the opposite of **certainty**.   **Knowledge** is the opposite of **ignorance**.

Every word in the grid below is an antonym of another word in the grid. Start with any word and draw a line to its antonym by passing through the empty squares. But you must move only vertically or horizontally, not diagonally, and none of your lines can cross. Use a pencil so you can erase. One line is drawn for you.

				serious	
plentiful	affirm				
			vague		
	arrogant		deny		
		comical		sparse	
clear			humble		

LANGUAGE LINES

Write the correct past tense form of the verb in parentheses to complete each sentence.

1. We _____ fresh-baked cookies to the picnic. **(bring)**

2. Emily _____ three new shirts to buy at the store. **(choose)**

3. John watched as the sun slowly _____ below the horizon. **(sink)**

4. Jeremy and Anna _____ a sand castle together. **(build)**

5. Katie couldn't go to the movies because she _____ a cold. **(catch)**

6. Mrs. Collins _____ you not to pick those flowers. **(tell)**

7. My sister and I _____ up slowly to the sleeping kitten. **(creep)**

8. I _____ the book from cover to cover. **(read)**

9. The doctor _____ a cure for the deadly disease. **(seek)**

10. Smoke billowed into the air as the fire _____ across the prairie. **(sweep)**

In My Own Words

If you could be any animal for one day, what animal would you be? What would you do on that day?

Mind Jigglers

Arachnids

A. The answer is **a big black spider**. Write three different questions. They can be funny or serious.

1. _____

2. _____

3. _____

B. Unscramble the names of places where most people would not want to find a spider.

RIHA _____

HEOS _____

DEB _____

DOSA _____

WHACSIND _____

CCAAKKPB _____

PUSO _____

STANP _____

C. Draw a path that shows how the spider can get to all 10 flies and back to the center of the web without crossing its own path.

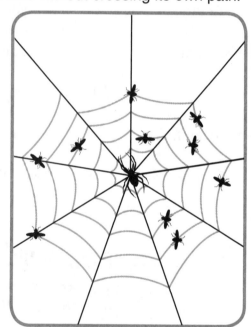

D. Finish the tongue twisters.

1. Sally the Spider saw _____

_____

2. Terry Tarantula tied _____

_____

MATH TIME

Elapsed Time

A. Complete the chart by filling in all the empty spaces.

Starting Time	Ending Time	Elapsed Time
7:15 AM	9:00 AM	
5:20 PM	6:15 PM	
11:00 AM	3:08 PM	
5:45 AM		2 hours, 20 minutes
8:42 PM		1 hour, 8 minutes
5:14 AM		5 hours, 55 minutes
	7:19 PM	2 hours, 7 minutes
	9:15 AM	1 hour, 47 minutes
5:19 AM	9:17 PM	
	8:15 PM	14 hours, 42 minutes

B. Solve the word problem.

Kayla's father said she had to clean her room before she could go to her friend's house. Kayla started cleaning at 10:15 AM. It took her 17 minutes to pick up her clothes and put them away neatly. She spent 24 minutes organizing her bookshelf. It took her 9 minutes to clean under her bed and 8 minutes to change her sheets. Then she spent 22 minutes vacuuming and dusting. Finally, Kayla was done and went to her friend's house.

1. How long did Kayla spend cleaning her room? _____

2. At what time did she go to her friend's house? _____

Africa's Bodies of Water

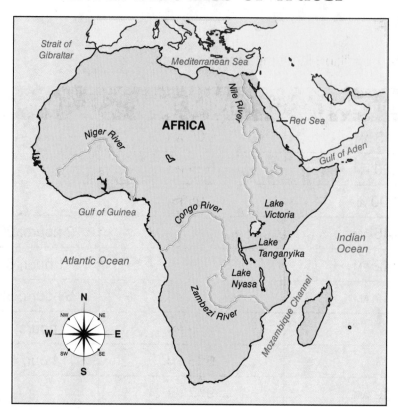

Use the map to answer the questions.

1. Which lake is the largest in Africa? _____

2. Which river is the longest in Africa? _____

3. Which sea is east of the Nile River? _____

4. Which river is farthest south? _____

5. Which body of water separates mainland Africa
   from its largest island? _____

6. Which two oceans border Africa?

   _____

West of Greenwich   Longitude West of Greenwich

120° B 150° C 180° D 150° E 120° F 90°

WEEK 4

Check off each box as you complete the day's work.

◻ **ALL WEEK**

◻ **MONDAY**

◻ **TUESDAY**

◻ **WEDNESDAY**

◻ **THURSDAY**

◻ **FRIDAY**

Spelling Words

assignment

campaign

handkerchief

moisten

mortgage

muscle

pneumonia

subtle

succumb

thistle

tomb

Wednesday

Get Creative!

Draw a picture to go with the speech bubble.

Oh no! I'm melting!

A Memorable Moment

What sticks in your mind about this week? Write about it.

_____

_____

_____

_____

_____

_____

_____

Reading Record

	Book Title	Pages	Time
Monday	_____	_____	_____
Tuesday	_____	_____	_____
Wednesday	_____	_____	_____
Thursday	_____	_____	_____
Friday	_____	_____	_____

Describe a character you read about this week.

_____

_____

_____

_____

_____

_____

Read the story. Then answer the questions.

Prometheus

In ancient Greek mythology, Prometheus was a Titan, one of the most powerful gods. Yet even though he was a god, he found humans interesting. Zeus, the ruler of all the gods, did not care about human struggles, but Prometheus wanted to help the mortals.

According to the myths, Prometheus looked for ways to help humans solve their problems. For example, he taught people how to make bricks to build homes, how to tell the seasons by looking at the stars, and how to navigate ships. Humans, with the help of Prometheus's knowledge, began to advance. They became more independent.

Zeus ordered Prometheus to stop helping the humans, but Prometheus continued. After Prometheus stole fire from Zeus and gave it to the people, Zeus grew incredibly angry. Until then, he alone had controlled fire. By giving it to the humans, Prometheus was offering them the final power they needed to grow and prosper without the help of the gods.

Zeus was furious. "You dared to defy me?" he cried. "You brought fire to those too foolish to use it properly. Now you must be punished!" Zeus chained Prometheus to a mountain and sent an eagle to tear at his flesh. While Prometheus remained bound and helpless, the eagle ate his liver. Each day, the liver grew back, and the eagle attacked it anew.

Prometheus's torture continued for years. Finally, brave Heracles, Zeus's son, could no longer stand to see Prometheus suffer. Heracles killed the eagle and set Prometheus free.

· ·

1. **Which of these statements best tells the main idea of the passage?**

   Ⓐ Zeus and Prometheus fought about Heracles.

   Ⓑ Zeus told Prometheus to avoid humans.

   Ⓒ Prometheus was chained to a mountain, and an eagle ate his liver.

   Ⓓ Prometheus disobeyed Zeus by sharing knowledge with humans.

2. **Which of these is the main idea of the second paragraph?**

   Ⓐ Prometheus wanted to see humans prosper.

   Ⓑ Prometheus thought humans were foolish.

   Ⓒ Zeus kept Prometheus away from humans.

   Ⓓ Prometheus helped humans, but they were ungrateful.

3. **Which detail explains why Zeus finally decided to punish Prometheus?**

   Ⓐ Prometheus gave fire to humans.

   Ⓑ Prometheus was a Titan.

   Ⓒ Prometheus taught humans to make bricks and build homes.

   Ⓓ Prometheus got help from Heracles.

4. **Which of these details shows that Prometheus's torture was ongoing?**

   Ⓐ Zeus chained Prometheus to a mountain.

   Ⓑ Prometheus's liver grew back, and the eagle attacked it repeatedly.

   Ⓒ Prometheus was bound and helpless.

   Ⓓ Heracles killed the eagle and freed Prometheus.

Write It Right

Rewrite each sentence, correcting the errors.

1. after we goes to the mall, than lets get sum Pizza

   _____

2. Look at all them children playing, in the fountin!

   _____

3. taylor and emily checks out sevin books at the libary yesterday

   _____

4. joshua asks me to goes to the dance last wensday

   _____

MATH TIME

Use the clues to find each number.

1. • This number is a mixed number. • When this number is multiplied by $\frac{3}{4}$, the product is $1\frac{1}{8}$. _____	2. • This number is a mixed number. • When this number is divided by $\frac{2}{5}$, the answer is $8\frac{1}{2}$. _____	3. • This number is a mixed number. • When this number is multiplied by $\frac{1}{3}$, the product is $1\frac{2}{5}$. _____

© Evan-Moor Corp. • EMC 1068 • Daily Summer Activities

SPELL IT

> Many words have consonants that are **silent**.
> For example, the **t** is silent in the word **hustle**.

Fill in the letters to complete the spelling words for the week. Then circle the silent consonant in each word.

1. sub_____

2. _____monia

3. mus_____

4. Wed_____

5. _____gage

6. to_____

7. _____ten

8. camp_____

9. _____kerchief

10. suc_____

11. thi_____

12. assign_____

In My Own Words

What is the best gift that you have ever received?
What made it so special?

LANGUAGE LINES

A group of words that expresses a complete thought is called a **sentence**. A group of words that does not express a complete thought is called a **fragment**.

Write *sentence* or *fragment* after each group of words.

1. Andrew went to the store with his mother.   _____

2. Ate lunch together in the cafeteria.   _____

3. My little brother and his friends from school.   _____

4. The mosquitoes, they were everywhere!   _____

5. We always go to the movies on Saturday.   _____

6. When all of the people in my neighborhood gather.   _____

7. Knows how to put together a kite.   _____

8. She ate.   _____

MATH TIME

Measure the length of each writing tool to the nearest quarter inch.

1.    _____ inches

2.    _____ inches

3.    _____ inches

4.    _____ inches

Read the article and study the diagram. Then answer the questions.

Parts of the Eye

The human eye is a remarkable system of sensitive parts. These tiny tissues work together to send messages to the brain.

First, light rays enter the eye through the transparent **cornea**. The rays then pass through the **pupil**, which changes size to adjust to different light levels. The pupil dilates, or becomes bigger, in dark rooms and will contract, or become smaller, in brightly lit places.

The **iris** is the colored part of the eye, and it controls the opening and closing of the pupil. Irises can be blue, green, brown, gray, or hazel.

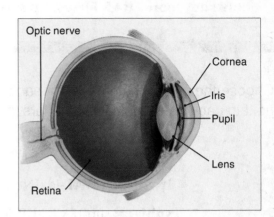

The **lens** focuses the light rays on the **retina**. The retina is tissue at the back of the eye that is sensitive to light. Nerves in the retina convert light energy into electrical energy, which is sent along the **optic nerve** to the brain. The brain interprets the electrical energy as an image.

. . . .

1. **What do the diagram labels identify?**

   Ⓐ six types of human eyes

   Ⓑ the parts of the human eye

   Ⓒ the functions of the optic nerve

   Ⓓ six diseases of the human eye

2. **In which chapter of a book about vision would you probably find the passage and diagram?**

   Ⓐ "Methods of Eye Examination"

   Ⓑ "History of Optics"

   Ⓒ "Infections of the Eye"

   Ⓓ "Anatomy of the Eye"

3. **According to the diagram, which parts of the eye are behind the lens?**

   Ⓐ the optic nerve and the retina

   Ⓑ the optic nerve and the pupil

   Ⓒ the retina, the pupil, the iris, and the cornea

   Ⓓ the retina and the cornea

4. **Why are some of the words in the passage in boldface?**

   Ⓐ They are difficult words to pronounce.

   Ⓑ They also appear in the diagram.

   Ⓒ They are part of the passage's main idea.

   Ⓓ They are important subheadings.

Vo·cab·u·lar·y

Heteronyms are words that are spelled the same but have different meanings and pronunciations. They can also be different parts of speech.

contract (con-TRAKT): (v.), "to shrink"   contract (CON-trakt): (n.), "an agreement"

Choose the correct heteronym for each pair of definitions. Then write the correct pronunciation next to each definition. Capital letters indicate emphasis.

> **digest:** dī-JEST, DĪ-jest   **permit:** pur-MIT, PUR-mit
>
> **invalid:** in-VAL-id, IN-vuh-lid   **perfect:** pur-FEKT, PUR-fikt
>
> **subject:** sub-JEKT, SUB-jekt   **console:** kun-SOHL, KON-sohl
>
> **entrance:** en-TRANSS, EN-trinss   **incense:** in-SENSS, IN-senss
>
> **minute:** mī-NOOT, MIN-it   **refuse:** ree-FYOOZ, REF-yooss

1. a substance that smells nice when burned *(n.)* _____

   to make angry *(v.)* _____

2. to spellbind *(v.)* _____

   where one enters *(n.)* _____

3. a sickly person *(n.)* _____

   not true or correct *(adj.)* _____

4. sixty seconds *(n.)* _____

   tiny *(adj.)* _____

5. to say no *(v.)* _____

   garbage *(n.)* _____

6. flawless *(adj.)* _____

   to make flawless *(v.)* _____

7. a collection of short articles or stories *(n.)* _____

   to process food *(v.)* _____

8. to allow *(v.)* _____

   a license *(n.)* _____

9. to give comfort *(v.)* _____

   the control unit of an electronic system *(n.)* _____

10. a topic or theme *(n.)* _____

    to expose to something *(v.)* _____

LANGUAGE LINES

A pronoun is used to replace a noun.

Read the paragraphs. Write the correct pronouns above the underlined words. The first one has been done for you.

                                        They

    Nicole and Aaron are at the library. <u>Nicole and Aaron</u> both have reports to finish. Nicole is writing about ancient Egypt for social studies. To start <u>Nicole's</u> research, Nicole read books about ancient Egypt. <u>Nicole</u> also watched a video about <u>ancient Egypt</u>. Aaron told Nicole that <u>Nicole</u> must be turning into an expert. She told <u>Aaron</u> that <u>Nicole</u> would like to visit Egypt.

    Aaron is writing about cats for science. Mrs. Armstrong, the librarian, brought Aaron and Nicole the books that <u>Aaron and Nicole</u> requested. <u>Mrs. Armstrong</u> explained that cats were important to the Egyptians. Aaron decided that <u>Aaron</u> would like to go to Egypt, too. Nicole told Aaron that <u>Aaron and Nicole</u> should go together. When I saw <u>Aaron and Nicole</u>, Nicole suggested that <u>Nicole, Aaron, and I</u> all go to Egypt. I said Egypt is too far away to travel to this afternoon!

In My Own Words

Describe your favorite place. Why do you like it so much? Use as much detail as you can.

Mind Jigglers

Ancient Rome

A. Rome had many emperors. A few are mentioned below. Read the clues, and then write the name of each emperor next to the years he was in power.

> • Nerva and Titus each ruled for fewer than 5 years.
>
> • Hadrian and Trajan ruled longer than the other emperors.
>
> • Nerva ruled just before Trajan.
>
> • Domitian's reign was longer than Vespasian's but shorter than Hadrian's.

AD **69—79:** _____   AD **96—98:** _____

AD **79—81:** _____   AD **98—117:** _____

AD **81—96:** _____   AD **117—138:** _____

B. Read this expression: *Rome wasn't built in a day.*

1. What do you think that expression means?

   _____

2. Give an example of when you might use that expression.

   _____

   _____

C. Complete the math problems.

1. Emperor Hadrian built a 73-mile-long wall during his reign. The wall took 8 years to build. About how many miles of wall were built each year? Round to the nearest whole number.

   _____ miles

2. Convert this Roman numeral to an Arabic numeral (the number system we use) to find out the year in which Rome was conquered.

   ## AD CDLXXVI

   Rome fell in AD _____.

MATH TIME

Circle Graph

There were 200 customers at the Soda Shop last Saturday. Mrs. McCool kept track of the number of people who bought each type of soda she sold. Here are the results:

Chocolate: 70 customers   **Root Beer:** 50 customers

Strawberry: 34 customers   **Vanilla:** 16 customers

Orange: 10 customers   **Cherry:** 20 customers

Use the information above to complete the circle graph and the key. Color each section of the graph a different color. Be sure the colors on your graph match the data and your key.

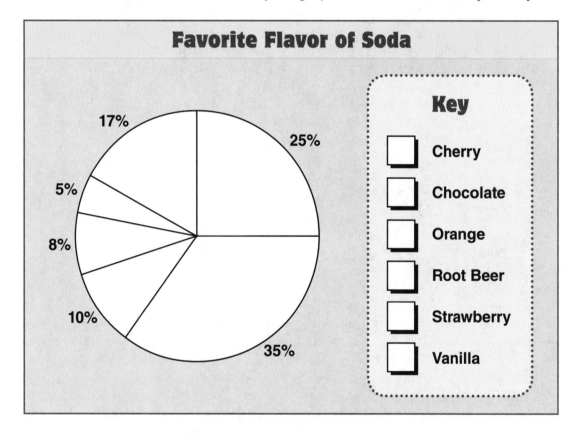

1. What percentage of customers purchased chocolate soda? _____

2. What percentage of customers purchased vanilla soda? _____

3. What is the difference in percentage between the largest and the smallest percent shown on the graph? _____

Geography

Most Populated Countries in Europe

Use the color key to color in each country. Then write a caption for the map, stating a fact about Europe's population.

Country	Population
European Russia	108,724,360
Germany	82,282,988
France	64,768,389
United Kingdom	61,284,806
Italy	58,090,681

Country	Population
Ukraine	45,415,596
Spain	40,548,753
Poland	38,463,689
Romania	22,181,287
Netherlands	16,783,092

Color Key
Largest population: **red**
Smallest population: **orange**
Populations 50 to 79 million: **green**
Populations 40 to 49 million: **blue**
Populations 20 to 39 million: **purple**
Country ranked second in population: **yellow**

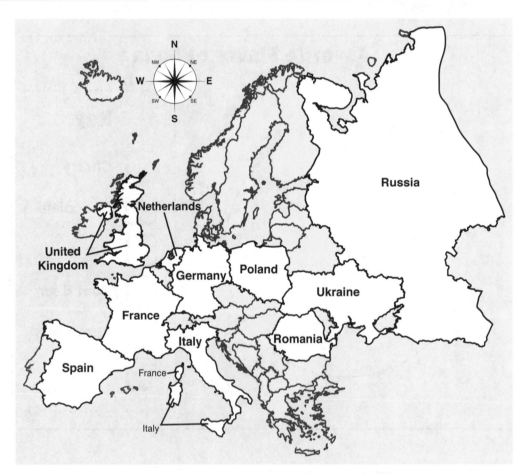

_____

_____

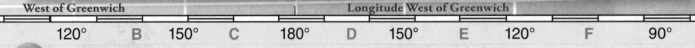

WEEK 5

Check off each box as you complete the day's work.

Spelling Words

administrator

choreographer

comedian

conductor

journalist

lawyer

librarian

magician

manager

orthodontist

physicist

professor

Get Creative!

Draw what you would see right now if you were standing on your head.

A Memorable Moment

What sticks in your mind about this week? Write about it.

_____

_____

_____

_____

_____

_____

Reading Record

	Book Title	Pages	Time
Monday	_____	_____	_____
Tuesday	_____	_____	_____
Wednesday	_____	_____	_____
Thursday	_____	_____	_____
Friday	_____	_____	_____

Describe a character you read about this week.

_____

_____

_____

_____

_____

_____

Read the journal entries. Then answer the questions.

The Whale Watch

Jeongsoo and Samuel went on a whale-watching trip to Cape Cod, Massachusetts, with their class. They each wrote an account of what they saw and did.

Jeongsoo's Account

I had looked forward to our Cape Cod whale-watching trip all year. When we finally got on the boat, I thought, "This is it!" After a year of studying everything about whales, we were finally going to see them. Being on the boat was great. It was sunny and windy, the waves were enormous, and it wasn't long before we noticed our first whale, a huge finback that spouted water up through its blowhole just a few feet from the boat. We saw 12 whales altogether, including minke whales, humpbacks, and the endangered right whale. And I got videos of them all on my cell phone! They were the most amazing creatures I'd ever seen.

Samuel's Account

All year our class had studied whales, and I worked really hard learning about them and about the ocean. I could hardly wait to see the whales in their own habitat, and I was excited when we finally got to the boat. The waves were huge, though, and when the boat started moving, I began to feel weird. Then I got nauseated—really, really nauseated. I spent the whole day miserable with seasickness, curled up in a chair inside the cabin. I heard everyone shouting as the whales breached and spouted, but I missed it all. Luckily, Jeongsoo filmed the whales with his cell phone, so I got to see his video. The whales really were awesome.

. . . .

1. **What is one similarity between Jeongsoo's and Samuel's experiences?**

   Ⓐ They both got really sick.

   Ⓑ They both had a great time.

   Ⓒ They both looked forward to the trip.

   Ⓓ They both sat in the ship's cabin.

2. **Samuel's time on the boat was different from Jeongsoo's because Samuel _____.**

   Ⓐ saw a whale spout

   Ⓑ did not see any whales during the trip

   Ⓒ had studied whales all year

   Ⓓ had a cell phone

3. **The boys both thought that the _____.**

   Ⓐ whales were amazing

   Ⓑ trip was fun

   Ⓒ boat movement was sickening

   Ⓓ humpback whale was huge

4. **Jeongsoo's experience was more enjoyable than Samuel's because Jeongsoo _____.**

   Ⓐ learned more about whales in school

   Ⓑ did not get sick

   Ⓒ went to Cape Cod

   Ⓓ had a better seat on the ship

Write It Right

Rewrite each sentence, correcting the errors.

1. No body couldn't tell us, wear the blew house was

_____

_____

2. may I please have some more potatos spinach and corn the little boy asked?

_____

_____

3. Mr and mrs tyler left for hawaii on friday august 25th and returned the following week

_____

_____

MATH TIME

Round each of these numbers to the specified place value.

1. 280 to the nearest hundred   _____

2. 49,305 to the nearest thousand   _____

3. 27,539 to the nearest ten   _____

4. 184,390 to the nearest ten thousand   _____

5. 286,952 to the nearest hundred thousand   _____

6. 1,682,842 to the nearest hundred thousand _____

7. 5,930,206 to the nearest million   _____

SPELL IT

The suffixes **–ian**, **–ist**, **–er**, and **–or** often mean "one who."
For example, a **florist** is "one who sells flowers."

Fill in the appropriate suffix for each of this week's spelling words.

1. conduct_____

2. journal_____

3. physic_____

4. choreograph_____

5. magic_____

6. manag_____

7. librar_____

8. administrat_____

9. orthodont_____

10. comed_____

11. profess_____

12. lawy_____

In My Own Words

What do you think your life will be like in 20 years?

LANGUAGE LINES

Words that measure weight, length, and volume are often written as **abbreviations**.

Write the letter of the correct abbreviation next to its measurement word.

_____ 1. pound

_____ 2. kilometer

_____ 3. milliliter

_____ 4. mile

_____ 5. centigram

_____ 6. quart

_____ 7. ounce

_____ 8. kilogram

_____ 9. liter

_____ 10. centimeter

a. mL

b. qt.

c. lb.

d. kg

e. L

f. cm

g. km

h. cg

i. oz.

j. mi.

MATH TIME

Solve each equation. Show all of your work. The first one has been done for you.

1. $x + 4 = 53$ $x =$ __49__
$x = 53 - 4$
$x = 49$

2. $x + 27 = 368$ $x =$ _____

3. $x + 18 = 12$ $x =$ _____

4. $(x + 5) + 5 = 11$ $x =$ _____

5. $x - 6 = 21$ $x =$ _____

6. $x - 15 = -4$ $x =$ _____

7. $x - 44 = 13$ $x =$ _____

8. $(x - 9) + 17 = 12$ $x =$ _____

Read the article. Then answer the questions.

Ray Wallace's Bigfoot Hoax

For decades, people have heard about sightings of a gigantic creature called Bigfoot in the forests of the Pacific Northwest. According to the stories, the creature always left huge footprints. A logger named Ray Wallace helped popularize these stories about Bigfoot.

In 1958, one of Wallace's workers reported to a newspaper that he had spotted the creature's tracks. Wallace explained that his workers were scared of the beast. The story spread, and some people connected the creature to other legendary monsters, especially the Abominable Snowman, or Yeti, said to live in the mountains of Nepal. Wallace had pictures and film footage of a huge, furry primate to back up his story. He also tried to sell castings of giant footprints and recordings of the creature's cries.

But in 2002, after Ray Wallace died, his family members had their own story to tell. They said that Wallace was a prankster and made the giant footprints himself. Wallace's wife admitted dressing up in a Bigfoot costume as part of the hoax. Apparently, Ray Wallace enjoyed fooling people. He told his Bigfoot stories for decades. However, Wallace certainly was not responsible for all the other reported sightings of Bigfoot. In fact, some people continue to report seeing the monster. Nonetheless, when Ray Wallace passed away, his own son said, "Bigfoot is dead."

. . . .

1. **In the passage, the author mainly tries to _____.**

   Ⓐ entertain readers with colorful tales about Bigfoot

   Ⓑ inform readers about a famous prank

   Ⓒ persuade readers that Wallace was a criminal

   Ⓓ instruct readers on how to create their own hoaxes

2. **Why does the author include the quotation from Wallace's son at the end of the passage?**

   Ⓐ to show that many still believe in Bigfoot

   Ⓑ to show how the son felt about his father's death

   Ⓒ to show that the son knows that his dad made up Bigfoot

   Ⓓ to persuade readers that Bigfoot once existed but is now dead

3. **Which detail might be true for Yeti, but not for Bigfoot?**

   Ⓐ It lives in Nepal.

   Ⓑ It is large and furry.

   Ⓒ Ray Wallace invented stories about it.

   Ⓓ People are frightened by it.

4. **Which of these is one theme of "Ray Wallace's Bigfoot Hoax"?**

   Ⓐ Many things in nature cannot be explained.

   Ⓑ Nature is filled with terrifying things.

   Ⓒ Secrets are safe with families, even after members of a family die.

   Ⓓ One person's monster may be another person's prank.

Vo·cab·u·lar·y

Synonyms are words that have almost the same meaning. You can use synonyms to vary your writing or to make your language more precise.

Pursue is a synonym for **chase**.
Confirm is a synonym for **prove**.

A. Write the letter of the correct synonym next to each word. Use a dictionary to help you.

_____ 1. happy

_____ 2. approve

_____ 3. burden

_____ 4. trespass

_____ 5. threaten

_____ 6. tempt

_____ 7. courageous

_____ 8. determination

a. encroach

b. entice

c. intimidate

d. endorse

e. valiant

f. elated

g. tenacity

h. encumber

B. For each word, find the synonym given for it above. Then write a sentence using the synonym.

1. **burden:** _____

_____

2. **tempt:** _____

_____

3. **happy:** _____

_____

4. **determination:** _____

_____

LANGUAGE LINES

Ryan, what time is it?   **It is three o'clock, Emma.**

Rewrite these sentences correctly, adding commas where they are needed.

1. Kaya have you finished your chores?

   _____

2. I think I have Ben.

   _____

3. Kaya let's get Dad to drive us to the mall.

   _____

4. Dad can you take Ben and me to the mall?

   _____

In My Own Words

Name a book you have read that you think should be made into a movie.
Why would this book make a good movie?

Mind Jigglers

Pioneer Days

All of the children in the Swenson family help around the farm. However, each child has a special chore that he or she must do. Read the clues and fill out the chart to find out who does each chore and how old each child is. Make an **X** in a space when it *cannot* be an answer. Draw a circle in a space when it is a correct answer. **Hint:** When you draw a circle in a space, you can make an **X** in all of the other spaces in that row and column.

		Chores						Ages					
		Do dishes	Do laundry	Milk cow	Collect eggs	Sweep floor	Chop wood	6	8	10	13	15	17
Children	Sarah												
	Jonah												
	Naomi												
	Charles												
	Mary												
	Jacob												
Ages	6												
	8												
	10												
	13												
	15												
	17												

1. The oldest children chop wood and do laundry.

2. The dishes and the laundry are both done by girls. A boy chops wood.

3. Both the youngest and the oldest children are boys.

4. Charles, who is 3 years younger than Sarah, collects eggs.

5. The youngest child sweeps the floor.

6. When Mary is done with her chores, she sometimes helps her youngest sister in the kitchen.

7. When Jacob was a baby, Mary used to help change his diapers.

© Evan-Moor Corp. • EMC 1068 • Daily Summer Activities

MATH TIME

Reducing Fractions

One way to reduce fractions to their lowest terms is to find the Greatest Common Factor (GCF) of the numerator and the denominator. Divide both fractions by the GCF and you have reduced them to lowest terms.

The GCF of 12 and 20 is 4. Divide both the numerator and denominator by 4.

$$\frac{12}{20} = \frac{12 \div 4}{20 \div 4} = \frac{3}{5}$$

Find the GCF of each numerator and denominator. Then reduce the fraction. The first one has been done for you.

	GCF	Reduced Fraction			GCF	Reduced Fraction
1. $\frac{3}{9} \div$	$\frac{3}{3}$	$= \frac{1}{3}$		6. $\frac{13}{39} \div$	_____	$=$ _____
2. $\frac{8}{12} \div$	_____	$=$ _____		7. $\frac{12}{15} \div$	_____	$=$ _____
3. $\frac{10}{25} \div$	_____	$=$ _____		8. $\frac{20}{24} \div$	_____	$=$ _____
4. $\frac{15}{20} \div$	_____	$=$ _____		9. $\frac{15}{60} \div$	_____	$=$ _____
5. $\frac{4}{50} \div$	_____	$=$ _____		10. $\frac{36}{42} \div$	_____	$=$ _____

© Evan-Moor Corp. • EMC 1068 • Daily Summer Activities

Geography

The Caribbean

In the Caribbean Sea, east of Central America, there are thousands of islands. Among these are 13 independent nations, as well as 11 territories. The Caribbean can be divided into three regions: the Bahamas, the Greater Antilles, and the Lesser Antilles.

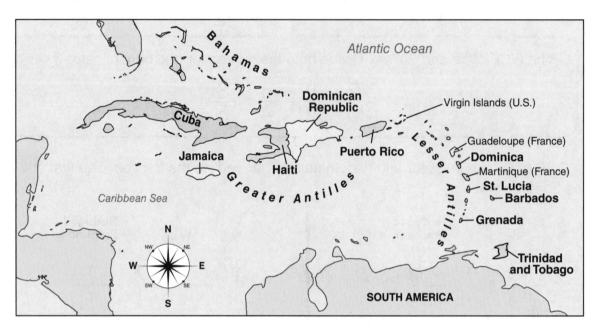

Read each statement. Circle *yes* if it is true or *no* if it is false. Use the map and the information above to help you.

1. There are 11 independent nations in the Caribbean.   Yes   No

2. The Virgin Islands are a U.S. territory.   Yes   No

3. Grenada is the closest island to South America.   Yes   No

4. Dominica is an island in the Lesser Antilles.   Yes   No

5. Martinique is part of the Greater Antilles.   Yes   No

6. Cuba is south of the Bahamas.   Yes   No

7. Puerto Rico is the farthest east of all the islands.   Yes   No

8. Guadeloupe is part of the Bahamas.   Yes   No

WEEK 6

Check off each box as you complete the day's work.

Spelling Words

anxious

beneficial

depression

discussion

distinction

especially

essential

intermission

obnoxious

potential

sufficient

transitional

Get Creative!

Draw a picture of a flower using only straight lines.

A Memorable Moment

What sticks in your mind about this week? Write about it.

_____

_____

_____

_____

_____

_____

_____

Reading Record

	Book Title	Pages	Time
Monday	_____	_____	_____
Tuesday	_____	_____	_____
Wednesday	_____	_____	_____
Thursday	_____	_____	_____
Friday	_____	_____	_____

Describe a character you read about this week.

_____

_____

_____

_____

_____

_____

Read the story. Then answer the questions.

A Wild Flamingo Chase

Rodney read the headline in the local paper: "Flamingo Flocks to Fern Fields." An exotic bird had found its way to Rodney's small California town. It was a flamingo, the report said, a real one—not like the faded, plastic version planted in Rodney's neighbor's yard. The town didn't even have a zoo, so this news was really exciting. But where was the bird? Rodney thought it would stick out like a sore thumb.

Only one man in town claimed to have seen the wild bird, in a wetland park on the outskirts of town. He described the flamingo's pink feathers and said it stood approximately 3 feet tall. He also said the flamingo did not seem sick or hurt.

Rodney thought the story sounded suspicious, though, so he decided to go on a flamingo-finding expedition. He also decided to take his best friend, Paul, with him. The boys assembled their gear—tall rubber boots, binoculars, and a camera. They packed some peanut butter sandwiches, too. Then they set out for the wetlands.

With boots up to their thighs, Rodney and Paul trudged through muck and mud for what seemed like an eternity, but they never spotted the flamingo. Finally the sun began to set, and a cold wind cut through the boys' jackets. Rodney and Paul decided to head home.

As they turned onto Paul's street, they saw Paul's mom waiting on the porch. Paul dragged his feet up the driveway. His mom put her arm around him, and the two went inside.

Rodney continued down the street toward his house, past his neighbor's yard and that ridiculous plastic pink flamingo. "Great," Rodney thought, "now there's a pair of them." Then, out of the corner of his eye, Rodney saw something move.

. . . .

1. **What is the author's purpose in this passage?**

   Ⓐ to tell you facts about flamingos

   Ⓑ to entertain you with a story about a boy looking for a flamingo

   Ⓒ to teach you how to study birds

   Ⓓ to persuade people not to study flamingos

2. **What will Paul probably tell his mom?**

   Ⓐ He will recall the dangers of walking through the wetlands.

   Ⓑ He will admit that they lost the sandwiches.

   Ⓒ He will express disappointment for not spotting the flamingo.

   Ⓓ He will say he is excited about being home.

3. **Why does the author say the flamingo is *exotic?***

   Ⓐ to let you know that the flamingo is not a native species

   Ⓑ to tell you how beautiful the flamingo is

   Ⓒ to tell you how costly the flamingo is

   Ⓓ to let you know that Rodney is intelligent

4. **Which of these is most likely to happen next?**

   Ⓐ Paul will go to Rodney's for dinner.

   Ⓑ Rodney will return to the wetlands.

   Ⓒ Rodney will put a flamingo in his yard.

   Ⓓ Rodney will look again at the flamingos on the lawn.

Write It Right

Rewrite each sentence, correcting the errors.

1. Lets all go too the carnival, "said james"

   _____

2. Brad and angie wood not share, they're chips with jennifer

   _____

3. I atend mark twain jr hi in redmond washington.

   _____

4. We goes to Jame's house after scool tommorrow

   _____

MATH TIME

Plot each of the following points on the number line and label them with the corresponding letters. The letters will spell out a favorite swimming activity.

$4\frac{1}{5}$	**A**	2.6	**C**
7.8	**O**	$9\frac{1}{2}$	**B**
$5\frac{1}{10}$	**N**	$11\frac{4}{5}$	**A**
$14\frac{3}{5}$	**L**	13.2	**L**
8.5	**N**	6.4	**N**

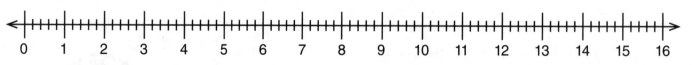

SPELL IT

The /**sh**/ sound is sometimes spelled **xi**, **ci**, **ti**, or **si**.

Fill in the correct letters that stand for the /**sh**/ sound in the spelling words for the week.

1. an_____ous

2. distinc_____on

3. suffi_____ent

4. essen_____al

5. obno_____ous

6. espe_____ally

7. transi_____onal

8. intermis_____on

9. discus_____on

10. benefi_____al

11. poten_____al

12. depres_____on

In My Own Words

Write about something you would like to invent that would make life easier for people.

LANGUAGE LINES

An **indefinite pronoun** is a pronoun that refers to an unspecified person or thing.

Circle the indefinite pronoun that correctly completes each sentence.

1. We need _____ to help out this weekend for the class cleanup.

    one   everybody   all

2. _____ have signed up for litter patrol in the park.

    Each   Several   Other

3. Surprisingly, _____ has volunteered yet to work at the beach.

    few   another   no one

4. _____ needs to pick up the trash there.

    Somebody   Both   Most

MATH TIME

Find the area of each polygon. **Reminder:** The area of a triangle is ½ (base x height).

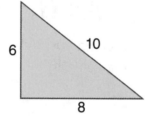

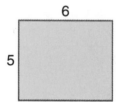

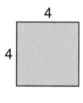

1. _____   2. _____   3. _____   4. _____

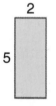

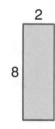

5. _____   6. _____   7. _____   8. _____

Read the article. Then answer the questions.

The Brigantines

The sailing ships on which pirates traveled the seas long ago were magnificent boats. This diagram shows one common type of ship they used, called the *brigantine*, or brig. Many pirates in the 1700s preferred the brig because it was light and fast. It also had a large cargo hold for plenty of pirates' loot!

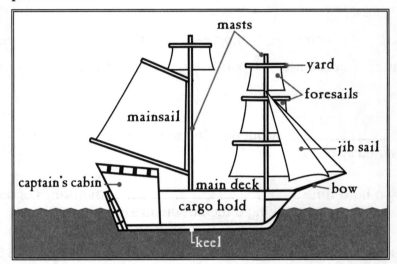

A brig is a "square-rigged" sailing ship, which means that the primary sails are at right angles to the length of the ship. They hang from strong horizontal poles called *yards*, which are at right angles to the mast.

· ·

1. **The main purpose of the passage is to _____.**

   Ⓐ interest readers in modern-day pirates

   Ⓑ teach important nautical terms

   Ⓒ describe a type of pirate ship and identify its parts

   Ⓓ stop readers from identifying pirates as heroes

2. **In the diagram, a *yard* is _____.**

   Ⓐ a place where brigs are kept

   Ⓑ a pole from which a sail is hung

   Ⓒ one of several sleeping quarters for the crew

   Ⓓ a unit of measurement for the size of a sail

3. **On a brig, the captain's cabin is _____.**

   Ⓐ near the rear of the ship

   Ⓑ just behind the bow

   Ⓒ entirely below the main deck

   Ⓓ just beneath the foresail

4. **According to the passage and diagram, a *mast* must be a _____.**

   Ⓐ type of sail

   Ⓑ type of boat

   Ⓒ famous pirate

   Ⓓ part of the ship

Vo·cab·u·lar·y

Using **precise language** makes your meaning clear and your writing more interesting.
Choose carefully among synonyms to make your writing more precise.

Write the word for *think* that best fits each definition in parentheses and completes the sentence.
Use a dictionary if necessary.

deduced	deems	suppose	theorizes	consider
imagining	assumes	pondering	hypothesized	contemplated

1. He _____ what decision to make for a long time.
   (thought seriously about)

2. We were having a hard time _____ thousands of buffalo on the plains.
   (making a mental picture of)

3. I'm not sure it's the best idea, but I _____ we could jump.
   (believe)

4. Dr. Smith _____ that the number of bugs was due to the heavy rain.
   (guesses or forms a theory)

5. Based on the evidence, I have _____ that the butler did it.
   (concluded)

6. I will _____ all my options before choosing a summer camp.
   (think carefully about)

7. Copernicus _____ that Earth revolves around the sun.
   (proposed an idea to explain facts)

8. I was _____ the meaning of the question all night.
   (thinking deeply about)

9. Mom _____ I have homework every night.
   (takes for granted)

10. Lin _____ that it's better to shower before bedtime than in the morning.
    (has an opinion)

LANGUAGE LINES

When the beginning sounds of several words in a phrase are the same, it is called **alliteration**.

Circle the words in each sentence that demonstrate alliteration.

1. Nobody knows how Nora's nicest shoes ended up in the puppy's bed.

2. The hazy, hot, humid weather made Henry Harvey feel like he was wrapped in a horribly heavy, wet blanket.

3. Sheila shouldn't show everyone Sean's photographs without his permission.

4. We have many merry memories of Emily's "musical madness" parties.

5. Stella stared at the stars on Saturday evening.

6. Poor Paul paraded around town in an old pair of pajamas.

In My Own Words

What are the qualities of a good friend?
Why are these things important?

Mind Jigglers

Supersize It!

A. List your answers to the following questions.

1. Besides the planet itself, what do you think are three of the biggest things in the world?

_____

_____

_____

2. What are three things that you wish were bigger than they are?

_____

_____

_____

B. Make up a question that could have the given answer. Write the question on the line.

1. The answer is **not very big**. What might the question be?

_____

2. The answer is **about as big as me**. What might the question be?

_____

C. Use the clues to name these big things.

"blank" of China: G_____ W_____

biggest mammal: b_____ w_____

large house: m_____

big meal: f_____

longest river: N_____

largest U.S. state: A_____

highest mountain: M_____ E_____

D. Will is 3 inches shorter than Karen. Karen is 2 inches taller than Jack. Jack is 4 inches taller than Grace. Will is 62 inches tall. How tall, in inches, is each child?

Will: _____

Grace: _____

Jack: _____

Karen: _____

MATH TIME

You Draw the Lines

On each figure, draw its lines of symmetry. If there are no lines of symmetry, write the word *none* next to the figure. If there are lines of symmetry, write the number of lines next to the figure.

1. 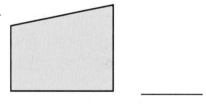 _____

2. 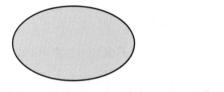 _____

3. 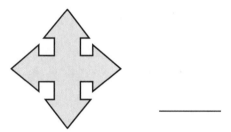 _____

4. 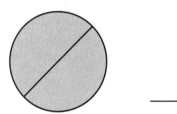 _____

5. 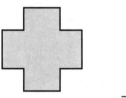 _____

6. 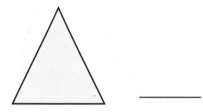 _____

7. 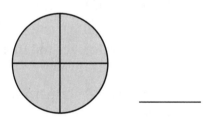 _____

8. 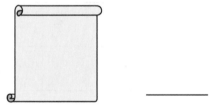 _____

Geography

Gold and Diamonds in Africa

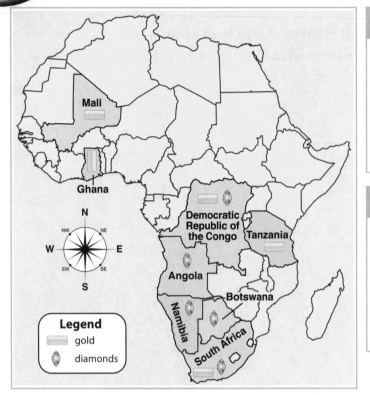

Legend
- gold
- diamonds

Top Five Gold Producers

1. South Africa
2. Ghana
3. Mali
4. Tanzania
5. Democratic Republic of the Congo

Top Five Diamond Producers

1. Botswana
2. Democratic Republic of the Congo
3. South Africa
4. Angola
5. Namibia

Use the map and the information above to answer the questions.

1. Which country is the second-highest producer of gold? _____

2. Which country is the highest producer of diamonds? _____

3. Which is the northernmost country that is a top producer of gold? _____

4. Which countries are top producers of both gold and diamonds?

    _____

5. Which countries are top producers of gold but not of diamonds?

    _____

West of Greenwich   Longitude West of Greenwich

A   120°   B   150°   C   180°   D   150°   E   120°   F   90°

WEEK 7

Check off each box as you complete the day's work.

Spelling Words

bouquet

bungalow

burrito

chandelier

delicatessen

finale

futon

gourmet

guitar

pajamas

sauerkraut

spaghetti

Get Creative!

Draw yourself as a cartoon character.

A Memorable Moment

What sticks in your mind about this week? Write about it.

_____

_____

_____

_____

_____

_____

_____

Reading Record

	Book Title	Pages	Time
Monday	_____	_____	_____
Tuesday	_____	_____	_____
Wednesday	_____	_____	_____
Thursday	_____	_____	_____
Friday	_____	_____	_____

Describe a character you read about this week.

_____

_____

_____

_____

_____

_____

© Evan-Moor Corp. • EMC 1002 • Daily Summer Activities

Read the story. Then answer the questions.

The Greedy Tiger and the Big Wind

Long ago, the rains did not fall, and there was a terrible drought. It was hard to find food, and the animals became hungry and thirsty. Only one tree had fruit. It was a big, beautiful pear tree that grew in the middle of a field. Its roots reached deep into the earth, where they drank from an underground spring. Its pears were plump and juicy. The tree, however, was guarded by a cruel and greedy tiger. Although he couldn't possibly eat all the fruit that the tree provided, Tiger wouldn't let any of the other animals touch the pears.

The desperate animals went to Rabbit and asked for help. Rabbit helped them form a plan. Then he went to Tiger and said, "Tiger, a great wind is coming. It will be so strong that it will blow everyone off the earth!" While Rabbit talked to Tiger, the birds, which were hidden in the forest, began to flap their wings wildly, creating a strong breeze. Next, other animals beat on the ground and swung through the trees, causing the trees to sway and shake. Tiger believed that the great wind had come, and he was terrified.

"I will tie you down with rope so the wind cannot blow you away," Rabbit offered. Tiger agreed, and Rabbit tied him tightly to a tree. Finally, Rabbit called the other animals, who came out of the forest and ate every delicious pear on the tree, laughing at the selfish tiger who watched helplessly.

. . . .

1. **The animals of the forest grew very hungry after _____.**

   Ⓐ Tiger ate all the juicy pears

   Ⓑ a drought came to the land

   Ⓒ the rains came to the land

   Ⓓ a great wind began to blow

2. **Before Rabbit tied up Tiger, the animals _____.**

   Ⓐ could not get to the pears

   Ⓑ ate all the pears

   Ⓒ laughed at Tiger

   Ⓓ came out of the forest

3. **What did Rabbit have to do before the animals could eat?**

   Ⓐ create a big wind

   Ⓑ make Tiger angry

   Ⓒ wait for the pears to ripen

   Ⓓ tie Tiger to a tree

4. **What happened after the animals made noise in the forest?**

   Ⓐ Tiger ran away in fear of the wind.

   Ⓑ Tiger allowed Rabbit to tie him up.

   Ⓒ Rabbit formed a plan.

   Ⓓ Rabbit warned Tiger about the wind.

Write It Right

Rewrite each sentence, correcting the errors.

1. marco and his little brother gone to the beech and builded sand cassles

   _____

2. When the piñata breaked all the childs runned to get the candy?

   _____

3. Lets wash the car and clean out the garage today. mother said

   _____

4. hanna and amy getted in to there moms jewelry draw

   _____

MATH TIME

Fill in the blanks to make each math sentence true.

1. 2 meters = _____ centimeters

2. 3 kilometers = _____ meters

3. 6 centimeters = _____ millimeters

4. 250 centimeters = _____ meters

5. 600 decimeters = _____ meters

6. 150 millimeters = _____ centimeters

7. 12 decimeters = _____ centimeters

8. $1\frac{3}{4}$ meters = _____ centimeters

9. 0.5 meters = _____ decimeters

10. 3 kilometers = _____ centimeters

11. 5.2 centimeters = _____ millimeters

12. 1.6 decimeters = _____ centimeters

SPELL IT

> Some English words are taken from other languages such as French, German, Spanish, and Hindu.

Circle the correct spelling for each of this week's spelling words.

1. pajamas   pajammas   pijammas

2. boquet   bouquet   bouquat

3. delicattesen   delicatessen   delicutessin

4. futon   fouton   futoun

5. spagetti   spaggeti   spaghetti

6. sauerkraut   saurkraut   sourkraut

7. chandileer   chandilier   chandelier

8. gormet   gourmet   gormat

9. burrito   buritto   burritto

10. guitaur   gitaur   guitar

11. bungallow   bungalow   bungalo

12. finaley   finalee   finale

In My Own Words

Describe the perfect meal. Use plenty of details to describe how it looks, smells, and tastes.

LANGUAGE LINES

Parentheses can be used to enclose extra information within a sentence.

Add parentheses in these sentences where they are needed.

1. Jan's cousins Barb and Bev who are also her best friends held a party for her 75th birthday.

2. Make an appointment for your driver's test at the local DMV Division of Motor Vehicles.

3. Please note that this bill must be paid in full within sixty 60 days.

4. Toni's favorite saying is "carpe diem" KAR-pay DEE-um, which means "seize the day."

5. Louisa May Alcott 1832–1888 wrote the novels *Little Women* and *Jo's Boys*.

6. Find the Lowest Common Denominator LCD of the numbers.

7. The number of languages currently spoken on the planet about 6,000 is decreasing.

8. The cartographers mapmakers of ancient times believed Earth was flat.

MATH TIME

A. Find the **range** of each set of data.

8, 5, 7, 8, 15, 23, 16 _____

42, 61, 51, 54, 59, 57, 60, 53, 61 _____

22, 24, 45, 31, 41, 38, 62, 26 _____

5, 16, 11, 19, 41, 20, 39, 24, 27, 25 _____

B. Find the **mean** of each set of data.

5, 8, 9, 11, 12, 15 _____

25, 26, 29, 31, 33, 35, 38, 39 _____

15, 18, 18, 19, 20, 23, 24, 25, 27 _____

7, 8, 9, 13, 14, 15, 16, 18, 26 _____

© Evan-Moor Corp. • EMC 1068 • Daily Summer Activities

Read the article. Then answer the questions.

The Cliff Dwellers

Mesa Verde, which means "green table" in Spanish, is the name of a high plateau in Colorado. Made of sandstone and shale, this plateau rises almost 2,000 feet above the surrounding land. The mesa has many canyons with streams and rivers running through them. At the tops of the rocky canyon walls, there are many overhangs and cave-like alcoves that have formed from water seeping into the sandstone.

People first came to Mesa Verde sometime around AD 550. These early inhabitants dug into the floors of the alcoves, creating what are now called pit houses. Around AD 750, people moved out of the pit houses in the canyon walls and built above-ground houses from mud and stone. Then, around the year 1200, they returned to the alcoves in the canyon walls.

Nobody knows why the people returned to the cliff pit houses. They may have feared attack from other groups and believed the alcoves offered better protection. They may have wanted better shelter from the wind and blistering sun. Whatever the reason, the cliff dwellers stayed less than a hundred years in the pit houses after they had moved back.

By 1300, the cliff dwellings had been abandoned, probably because of a severe drought in the area. It wasn't until over four hundred years later that cowboys, trappers, and prospectors began to visit and photograph Mesa Verde, astonished by the sight of hundreds of cliff houses built into the walls of the canyons.

· ·

1. **According to the passage, which event happened last?**

   Ⓐ Mesa Verde inhabitants created pit houses.

   Ⓑ Water seeped into the rock and created alcoves.

   Ⓒ Cowboys, trappers, and prospectors learned of the cliff dwellings.

   Ⓓ Cliff dwellers abandoned the canyon walls because of drought.

2. **What kind of homes did the Mesa Verde inhabitants first build?**

   Ⓐ pit houses

   Ⓑ cave houses

   Ⓒ stone and mud houses

   Ⓓ wooden houses

3. **The Mesa Verde inhabitants returned to the alcoves in canyon walls _____.**

   Ⓐ before AD 550

   Ⓑ around AD 750

   Ⓒ around 1200

   Ⓓ after 1300

4. **What were the last homes that the Mesa Verde people inhabited?**

   Ⓐ cliff tops

   Ⓑ pit houses

   Ⓒ stone and mud houses

   Ⓓ wooden houses

Vo·cab·u·lar·y

A **blended word** is created by combining parts of two or more words into one word. Blended words are also called "portmanteau words." A *portmanteau* is a suitcase that opens into two compartments.

A. Write the blended word that matches each clue.

> picture + element = **pixel**   spoon + fork = **spork**
>
> emotion + icon = **emoticon**   pulse + quasar = **pulsar**
>
> guess + estimate = **guesstimate**   television + marathon = **telethon**
>
> cybernetic + organism = **cyborg**   documentary + drama = **docudrama**
>
> information + commercial = **infomercial**   simultaneous + broadcast = **simulcast**

1. a symbol that shows emotion in e-mails   _____

2. an artificial human   _____

3. a show on TV that explains a product   _____

4. a rotating star that emits pulsing waves   _____

5. a long fundraiser on TV   _____

6. broadcast live on both TV and radio simultaneously   _____

7. an estimate based on a guess   _____

8. one tiny unit of an image on a computer   _____

9. a spoon-shaped eating utensil with fork-like prongs   _____

10. a TV or movie dramatization based on facts   _____

B. Write the blended word for each pair of words. Use a dictionary to help you, if necessary.

1. modulation + demodulation =   _____

2. sports + broadcast =   _____

3. fan + magazine =   _____

4. smoke + fog =   _____

LANGUAGE LINES

Use **commas** to separate three or more items in a series.

Correct the sentences by adding commas where they are needed.

1. A human being's five senses are sight hearing touch taste and smell.

2. The cornea the pupil and the lens are three parts of the human eye.

3. The muscle known as the iris the jelly-like substance called vitreous fluid and the thumbnail-sized retina are other important eye parts.

4. The three main parts of the human ear are the canal the eardrum and the cochlea.

5. Hearing can be damaged by loud sounds, such as those made by jet planes jackhammers and highly amplified musical instruments.

6. A bacterial infection a viral infection or even an allergy can cause earaches.

In My Own Words

If you could control the weather, what would you do? Explain why.

Mind Jigglers

Invention Convention

A. Answer the questions to complete this sentence:
What has not yet been invented that would…

change how we travel to places? _____

make life easier at home? _____

be good for the planet? _____

change how we communicate? _____

be kind of silly? _____

B. What are three traits that an inventor should have?

1. _____

2. _____

3. _____

C. Take a guess. In what year do you think each object was invented?

ballpoint pen _____

vacuum cleaner _____

zipper _____

dishwasher _____

safety pin _____

stapler _____

Now do Activity D to see when they were actually invented.

D. Look at the dates listed below. Then use the clues to figure out what year each object was invented.

- The ballpoint pen was invented before the zipper.

- The safety pin and the vacuum cleaner were both invented in years that end in 9.

- The dishwasher was invented 2 years before the ballpoint pen.

- The stapler was invented 8 years after the vacuum cleaner.

1849: _____

1869: _____

1877: _____

1886: _____

1888: _____

1891: _____

MATH TIME

What's My Number?

Use the clues to find each number.

1. • My number is a mixed number.
   • When my number is multiplied by $\frac{3}{4}$, the product is $1\frac{1}{8}$.   _____

2. • My number is a mixed number.
   • When my number is divided by $\frac{2}{5}$, the answer is $8\frac{1}{2}$.   _____

3. • My number is a mixed number.
   • When my number is multiplied by $\frac{1}{3}$, the product is $1\frac{2}{5}$.   _____

4. • My number is *not* a mixed number.
   • When my number is divided by $\frac{1}{3}$, the answer is $1\frac{1}{2}$.
   • The numerator of my number is 1.   _____

Geography

East Asia

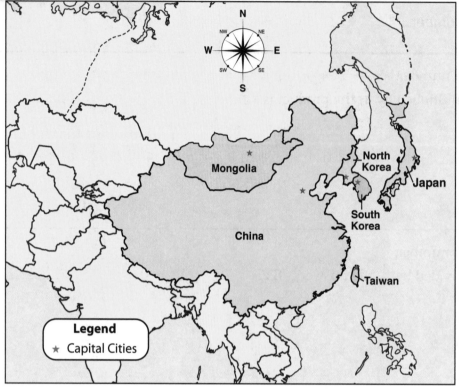

Country	Capital
China	Beijing
South Korea	Seoul
Japan	Tokyo
North Korea	Pyongyang
Taiwan	Taipei
Mongolia	Ulaanbaatar

Use the map and the chart to answer the questions.

1. Which country is north of China?   _____

2. What is the capital of Japan?   _____

3. What is the capital of Taiwan?   _____

4. Which four countries are east of China?

_____

5. What are the capitals of North Korea and South Korea?

_____

WEEK 8

Check off each box as you complete the day's work.

Spelling Words

beachcomber

downstream

eyewitness

featherweight

granddaughter

headquarters

laughingstock

overemphasize

straightforward

thundershower

underpopulated

wheelbarrow

Get Creative!

Make this letter into a picture.

W

A Memorable Moment

What sticks in your mind about this week? Write about it.

_____

_____

_____

_____

_____

_____

_____

Reading Record

	Book Title	Pages	Time
Monday	_____	_____	_____
Tuesday	_____	_____	_____
Wednesday	_____	_____	_____
Thursday	_____	_____	_____
Friday	_____	_____	_____

Describe a character you read about this week.

_____

_____

_____

_____

_____

_____

Read the journal entry. Then answer the questions.

Jesse's Journal

August 12

I'm so thankful we're all okay. I never imagined I'd have to go through something as terrifying as what happened yesterday. At first I thought we were about to have a regular thunderstorm. The sky got dark and the wind picked up. Dad came in early from the fields on his tractor. Then my sister Julia said, "Look at the sky. Doesn't it look weird?"

We went to the window and saw strange, heavy clouds. The sky had an eerie yellowish tint. I heard the wind begin to roar and started to feel frightened. Mom told us to run to the storm cellar, but I wanted to go to my room to get some of my things first. Mom grabbed me and made me stay with everyone else. As we ran toward the storm cellar, I saw a long, thin cloud drop down from the sky and touch the ground. The noise grew louder, like a train rushing straight at us. My little brother Mark started to cry. I picked him up and carried him down the steps into the cellar.

We turned on the emergency lamps and huddled together. Above us, we heard horrible sounds of crashing and tearing that seemed to go on forever. All I could think about was losing my computer and MP3 player. I knew Julia was worried about the clothes she had just bought, and Mark was thinking about his favorite toys.

When it finally grew quiet again, we came upstairs. The whole house was gone—just gone. The garage next to the house hadn't been touched, and the barn was fine. We all had the exact same reaction. Instead of crying about what we had lost, we hugged each other and cried because everyone was safe. We still had what mattered most—our family.

· ·

1. **When the tornado hits, what do the family's children think about most?**

   Ⓐ the cars and farm equipment

   Ⓑ their belongings

   Ⓒ their home

   Ⓓ their pets and farm animals

2. **How do you think Jesse feels about storms?**

   Ⓐ They are part of the natural world.

   Ⓑ They are symbols of spring and rebirth.

   Ⓒ They remind you that life can change quickly.

   Ⓓ They are minor annoyances that are soon forgotten.

3. **After the storm, why does the family cry?**

   Ⓐ They are thankful to be safe.

   Ⓑ They know they have to rebuild their house.

   Ⓒ They are very frightened.

   Ⓓ They are sad about losing their belongings.

4. **Which statement is a theme of the passage?**

   Ⓐ There is no love like a mother's love.

   Ⓑ Family is the most important thing.

   Ⓒ Taking care of your possessions is important.

   Ⓓ Fear can make bad events better.

Write It Right

Rewrite each sentence, correcting the errors.

1. wear did you find all of them tomatos carrots and, onions.

   _____

2. before diner I always help set the tabel, afterword I help clean up

   _____

3. I did'nt get no candie, when I went to the groshery store.

   _____

4. I no that you where going throu my stuff accused roxy.

   _____

MATH TIME

Use the information on the list to answer the questions.

1. How much did Ms. Boomer spend   _____
   on her Hawaiian vacation?

2. To pay for her vacation, Ms. Boomer   _____
   saved $175.00 a month for a year.
   After her vacation, how much of
   her savings did she have left?

3. How much did Ms. Boomer spend   _____
   on transportation?

4. If Ms. Boomer stayed at a hotel for   _____
   four nights, what was the nightly
   rate for her room?

Hawaiian Vacation Expenses

$750.83 Airfare

$600.48 Hotel

$195.00 Car rental

 $39.80 Souvenirs

$150.00 Scuba diving
         and surfing

$320.00 Meals

 $40.75 Park entrance fees

A **compound word** is made by
joining two smaller words.

Rewrite each of this week's spelling words correctly. Then draw a line between the two words
that make up each compound word.

1. laughinstock: _____

2. eyewittnes: _____

3. straigtforward: _____

4. grandaughter: _____

5. downstreem: _____

6. underpoppulated: _____

7. beachcomer: _____

8. tundersshower: _____

9. fetherwate: _____

10. wheelbarow: _____

11. hedquarters: _____

12. overremphacize: _____

In My Own Words
Do you think parents should limit the amount of time that kids play video games
and watch TV? Why or why not?

LANGUAGE LINES

A **subject** and a **verb** must agree in number.

Circle the correct form of the verb. Write whether the subject is *singular* or *plural* on the line.

1. Cat shows are large events that **attracts/attract** many pet owners. _____

2. I **enters/enter** my cat in the house-pet category. _____

3. Special breeds **competes/compete** in a different category. _____

4. A judge gently **examines/examine** a cat's bushy tail. _____

5. My cat **yawns/yawn** as she waits her turn. _____

6. The other cats **prances/prance** around the ring. _____

MATH TIME

Meredith and Derek were playing the probability game with marbles. Derek put 2 pink marbles, 6 blue marbles, and 16 green marbles in a bag. What is the probability of Meredith randomly selecting a marble that is...?

1. pink _____ 1 in 12 _____

2. blue _____

3. green _____

4. pink or blue _____

5. pink or green _____

6. blue or green _____

Read the passage and map. Then answer the questions.

Mesoamerica Before the Spanish

Long before the Spanish invaded Central America, a number of civilizations existed in the area now known as Mesoamerica. The map and timeline below provide dates and locations of a few of these extraordinary cultures.

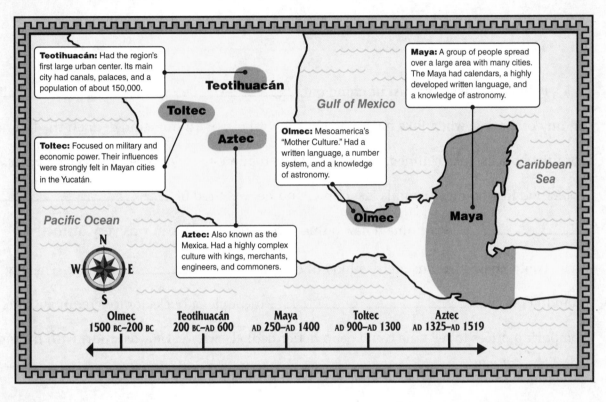

Teotihuacán: Had the region's first large urban center. Its main city had canals, palaces, and a population of about 150,000.

Toltec: Focused on military and economic power. Their influences were strongly felt in Mayan cities in the Yucatán.

Aztec: Also known as the Mexica. Had a highly complex culture with kings, merchants, engineers, and commoners.

Maya: A group of people spread over a large area with many cities. The Maya had calendars, a highly developed written language, and a knowledge of astronomy.

Olmec: Mesoamerica's "Mother Culture." Had a written language, a number system, and a knowledge of astronomy.

Gulf of Mexico

Caribbean Sea

Pacific Ocean

Teotihuacán · Toltec · Aztec · Olmec · Maya

N W E S

Olmec
1500 BC–200 BC

Teotihuacán
200 BC–AD 600

Maya
AD 250–AD 1400

Toltec
AD 900–AD 1300

Aztec
AD 1325–AD 1519

1. **Which two cultures did *not* exist around the same time?**

   Ⓐ the Teotihuacán and the Maya

   Ⓑ the Toltec and the Olmec

   Ⓒ the Toltec and the Maya

   Ⓓ the Aztec and the Maya

2. **According to the information on the map, which two cultures are known for their use of written language?**

   Ⓐ the Aztec and the Maya

   Ⓑ the Olmec and the Maya

   Ⓒ the Toltec and the Olmec

   Ⓓ the Teotihuacán and the Aztec

3. **Which culture extended the farthest south?**

   Ⓐ the Maya

   Ⓑ the Olmec

   Ⓒ the Teotihuacán

   Ⓓ the Aztec

4. **What information can be found on the map?**

   Ⓐ the boundaries of modern-day Mexico

   Ⓑ where the Spanish landed in 1519

   Ⓒ where each pre-1519 culture was located

   Ⓓ which countries the Spanish conquered

Vo·cab·u·lar·y

Fill in the blanks with the correct idioms.

fork over	wash his hands of	hook, line, and sinker
tightfisted	shooting the breeze	paying through the nose
way off base	gave him the lowdown	feeling like a million bucks

Pablo and Jake were just hanging out, _____ like

on any other day, when Jake mentioned he'd heard about an amazing deal on the Internet.

For thirty bucks, Jake claimed, anyone could be a game-tester and get free video games. Now,

Pablo had just spent $60 on his last game, and he was tired of _____

_____ every time a new game came out, so this idea was very attractive.

Pablo knew Jake was pretty stingy and _____. The guy

wouldn't even _____ a couple of bucks for ice cream without

comparing prices to see if he could get a better deal elsewhere. He was smart with his money,

so Pablo believed that this deal had to be a sure thing.

Jake helped Pablo register online and _____ on

how the program worked. Within hours, Pablo had received a gazillion e-mails trying to sell

him a gazillion things, but no games to test, and nothing free.

"Huh!" said Jake. "I guess I was _____ on this one."

As it turned out, the whole thing was a scam, and the boys had fallen for it _____

_____ .

Fortunately, Pablo was able to change his e-mail address and _____

_____ the entire mess. But he was still out $30. And instead of happily playing

free video games and _____, he simply felt like an idiot.

LANGUAGE LINES

Some nouns have unusual, or **irregular**, plural forms.

Write the plural form of each noun. Use a dictionary to help you, if necessary.

1. deer _____   6. alumnus _____   11. loaf _____

2. leaf _____   7. moose _____   12. cactus _____

3. hoof _____   8. crisis _____   13. shelf _____

4. woman _____   9. criterion _____   14. ox _____

5. louse _____   10. person _____   15. sheep _____

In My Own Words

What do you think are the five most important jobs in the world? Why are each of these jobs so important?

Mind Jigglers

From Here to There

Write the names of the towns you would visit on each route to Grandma's house. Then write the total number of miles you would travel.

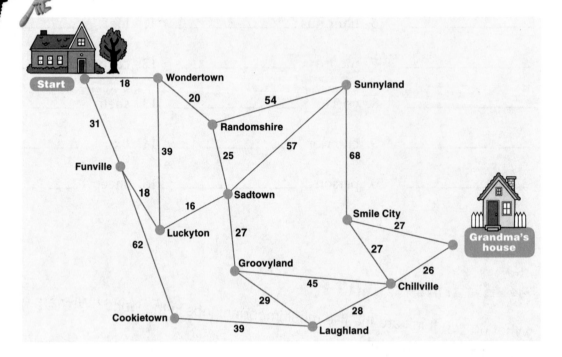

1. If you wanted to get there in the fewest miles possible, you would go through...

_____

_____ Total miles: _____

2. If you were on a bike and couldn't travel more than 30 miles each day, you would go through...

_____

_____ Total miles: _____

3. If you wanted to visit Groovyland but avoid Sadtown on the way, you would go through...

_____

_____ Total miles: _____

4. If you wanted to visit 11 towns before you got to Grandma's house, but you did not want to visit any town more than once, you would go through...

_____

_____ Total miles: _____

MATH TIME

Exponents

exponent
— 2
5^2

base

The large number is called a *base*.

The small number is called an *exponent*.

It shows how many times the base is used as a factor.

5^2 is read as "five squared."
It tells you to multiply 5 by itself two times.
$5 \times 5 = 25$

4^3 is read as "four cubed."
It tells you to multiply 4 by itself three times.
$4 \times 4 \times 4 = 64$

2^5 is read as "two to the fifth power."
It tells you to multiply 2 by itself five times.
$2 \times 2 \times 2 \times 2 \times 2 = 32$

A. Solve these problems using exponents.

1. $4^2 =$ _____

2. $2^3 =$ _____

3. $3^5 =$ _____

4. $8^2 =$ _____

5. $4^5 =$ _____

6. $5^3 =$ _____

7. $2^4 =$ _____

8. $6^3 =$ _____

B. Solve these equations using exponents.

1. $2^2 + 3^3 =$ _____

2. $6^2 + 4^3 =$ _____

3. $6^3 - 4^2 =$ _____

4. $3^2 - 2^3 =$ _____

5. $5^2 \times 3^3 =$ _____

6. $3^3 \times 3^2 =$ _____

7. $3^3 \div 3^2 =$ _____

8. $5^4 \div 5^2 =$ _____

© Evan-Moor Corp. • EMC 1068 • Daily Summer Activities

Geography

Countries of South America

South America is made up of 12 countries. Brazil is by far the largest in size, and Suriname is the smallest. In addition to the 12 independent countries, South America also has two dependencies, or territories. They are French Guiana and the Falkland Islands.

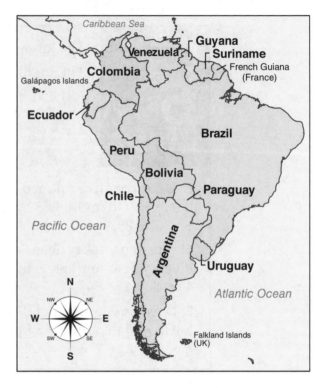

Read each statement. Circle *yes* if it is true or *no* if it is false. Use the information and the map above to help you.

1. Suriname is the largest country in South America.   Yes   No

2. There are two dependencies in South America.   Yes   No

3. Peru is west of Brazil.   Yes   No

4. Bolivia and Paraguay do not border an ocean.   Yes   No

5. The Pacific Ocean is east of Chile.   Yes   No

6. Brazil borders every South American country except Ecuador and Chile.   Yes   No

7. Bolivia is south of Argentina.   Yes   No

WEEK 9

Check off each box as you complete the day's work.

Spelling Words

accessible

adjustable

believable

compatible

convertible

eligible

exchangeable

inconsolable

invincible

maneuverable

negotiable

responsible

Get Creative!

Draw two faces with two opposite expressions.

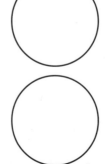

A Memorable Moment

What sticks in your mind about this week? Write about it.

_____

_____

_____

_____

_____

_____

_____

Reading Record

Book Title	Pages	Time
Monday _____	_____	_____
Tuesday _____	_____	_____
Wednesday _____	_____	_____
Thursday _____	_____	_____
Friday _____	_____	_____

Describe a character you read about this week.

_____

_____

_____

_____

_____

_____

Read the story. Then answer the questions.

Tamale Pie

"Open the tomatoes and corn," said Rosa's mom, Mrs. Chavez. "I'll chop the onions."

"Good," said Rosa. "Onions make me cry."

"Grind the walnuts," Mrs. Chavez ordered.

"I'm not sure the other Girl Scouts are going to like our tamale pie," said Rosa as she put the nuts into the grinder.

"Don't be silly," said Mrs. Chavez. "It's Cinco de Mayo, and this is a delicious recipe."

"But most people expect the main dish to have meat," Rosa said, concerned.

"Nuts are healthier. Now, shred the cheese." Mrs. Chavez put milk and cornmeal into a pot.

Two hours later, just as Rosa placed the tamale pie on the table, her dog Chivo started barking. "Hush!" said Rosa, heading to the door. "It's just my friends!"

Becca entered the kitchen. "Something smells great! I brought a bag of chips and some guacamole, but I don't know about the guacamole—it sort of turned brown."

Dede walked in, uncertain about her refried beans. Kari brought some cold quesadillas, Jenna brought slices of mango, and Cinder offered another bag of chips.

"The table's all set, and the tamale pie is ready," said Rosa. "Let's eat."

Steam and the smell of corn and tomatoes rose from the edges of the golden brown pie. "Wow!" the girls said at the same time. "It smells delicious!"

"There's no meat in it," Rosa said nervously.

"Who cares?" said Cinder. "Will you teach us how to cook, Mrs. Chavez?"

· ·

1. **In the future, Rosa will probably _____.**
   - Ⓐ refuse to cook with her mom
   - Ⓑ keep helping her mom prepare food
   - Ⓒ chop the onions for her mom
   - Ⓓ sneak meat into vegetarian recipes

2. **How will the girls most likely react after they taste the tamale pie?**
   - Ⓐ They will tell Rosa it should have meat in it.
   - Ⓑ They will decide not to eat it.
   - Ⓒ They will eat it and enjoy it.
   - Ⓓ They will add more seasoning.

3. **One of the Girl Scouts' next events will probably be _____.**
   - Ⓐ a dog-training class
   - Ⓑ a Cinco de Mayo party
   - Ⓒ cooking lessons with Mrs. Chavez
   - Ⓓ a camping trip to Mexico

4. **When the Girl Scouts are offered vegetarian food in the future, they will probably _____.**
   - Ⓐ want to try it
   - Ⓑ refuse to eat it
   - Ⓒ ask if they can add meat to it
   - Ⓓ offer to buy bags of chips instead

Write It Right

Rewrite each sentence, correcting the errors.

1. I think we should use the red white and blew rapping paper?

_____

2. My Aunt took a towel sum sun scream, a book and a apple to the beech

_____

3. Even thou John raysed his hand politely the teacher did'nt call on him

_____

4. Dad can you pickup Carolyn and I from skool tommorrow.

_____

MATH TIME

Use <, >, or = to make each math sentence true.

1. $\frac{3}{4}$ _____ $\frac{5}{7}$

2. $\frac{8}{12}$ _____ $\frac{2}{3}$

3. $1\frac{4}{5}$ _____ $\frac{8}{5}$

4. $3\frac{1}{3}$ _____ $\frac{11}{3}$

5. $\frac{5}{9}$ _____ $\frac{8}{13}$

6. $\frac{7}{10}$ _____ $\frac{4}{7}$

7. $4\frac{6}{7}$ _____ $\frac{34}{7}$

8. $\frac{2}{3} \times \frac{4}{5}$ _____ $\frac{7}{15}$

9. $\frac{1}{6}$ _____ $\frac{2}{9} \times \frac{3}{4}$

10. $\frac{4}{9} \times \frac{3}{10}$ _____ $\frac{3}{4} \times \frac{8}{15}$

SPELL IT

> The suffixes **–able** and **–ible** form adjectives that mean "likely to," "can be," or "worthy of."

Fill in the correct suffix, either *–ible* or *–able*, to complete the spelling words for the week.

1. access_____

2. convert_____

3. maneuver_____

4. respons_____

5. adjust_____

6. invinc_____

7. negoti_____

8. believ_____

9. elig_____

10. inconsol_____

11. exchange_____

12. compat_____

In My Own Words

If you could make up one law that everyone in the world must follow, what law would it be? Why?

LANGUAGE LINES

Quotation marks are used to show dialogue, or what someone has said.

Rewrite these sentences to correctly punctuate the dialogue. The first one has been done for you.

1. How are we going to get all these dishes washed Martina wondered?

   <u>"How are we going to get all these dishes washed?" Martina wondered.</u>

2. Lou called out I'll be waiting for you at the bus stop tomorrow!

   _____

3. No. Barbara repeated I don't know where the hammer is

   _____

4. I want to take an X-ray of your arm. the doctor told his patient.

   _____

5. Do you want to try to solve these equations together Mary asked?

   _____

MATH TIME

Solve each word problem.

1. Tim ran 100 yards in 21 seconds, and Juan ran 100 feet in 8 seconds. Who was running faster and why?

   _____

   _____

2. Frances walked 10 meters while Darcy walked 1,200 centimeters. Who walked farther? Why?

   _____

   _____

© Evan-Moor Corp. • FMC 1068 • Daily Summer Activities

Read the article. Then answer the questions.

The Man Who Loved the Sea

Jacques Cousteau was born in France in 1910. Although he was sickly as a child, he learned to swim at an early age and developed a love for the ocean. He joined the French navy in 1933, and it was there that he first used a pair of underwater goggles. Amazed at what he saw beneath the sea, he decided to build a device that would allow people to breathe underwater. In 1942, he finished the Aqua-Lung, a piece of early underwater breathing equipment that would eventually lead to the SCUBA diving gear used today.

After World War II, Cousteau began his life's work onboard the research ship *Calypso*. He worked with divers and scientists to photograph and gather samples of underwater plants and animals. In doing so, he learned about many ocean creatures that had never been studied before.

In 1960, he successfully worked to stop nuclear waste from being dumped into the Mediterranean Sea. He worked tirelessly to improve the ecological conditions of the world's oceans and won many awards for his efforts. His television show, *The Undersea World of Jacques Cousteau,* ran from 1968 to 1976. The series helped raise awareness of the creatures who inhabit the world's oceans. Cousteau died in 1997 at the age of 87 and is still celebrated as one of the most important explorers and environmentalists of the twentieth century.

· ·

1. **Which of these happened before Jacques Cousteau joined the navy?**

   Ⓐ He worked on the *Calypso*.

   Ⓑ He learned to swim.

   Ⓒ He had a television series.

   Ⓓ He won many awards.

2. **After World War II, what did Cousteau do?**

   Ⓐ He began using underwater goggles.

   Ⓑ He became very ill.

   Ⓒ He worked on the *Calypso*.

   Ⓓ He joined the navy.

3. **Cousteau developed the Aqua-Lung _____.**

   Ⓐ after joining the navy

   Ⓑ while working on the *Calypso*

   Ⓒ after winning awards

   Ⓓ before learning to swim

4. **Which of these events happened last?**

   Ⓐ Cousteau built an underwater breathing device.

   Ⓑ Cousteau protested against dumping nuclear waste.

   Ⓒ Cousteau joined the French navy.

   Ⓓ Cousteau's TV show raised awareness of the world's oceans.

Vo·cab·u·lar·y

A **base word** is a word that can stand alone before prefixes, suffixes, or other word parts are added.

keeping   un**happy**
careful   pre**view**

A. Write the base word of each word below. Watch out for spelling changes.

1. unbelievable _____

2. forgetful _____

3. dismissed _____

4. uncertainty _____

5. beautiful _____

6. timidity _____

7. carelessly _____

8. nonsensical _____

B. Complete each sentence by writing a base word from Activity A on the line.

1. Do not _____ to return your library book.

2. Tim felt nervous and _____ about giving his class presentation.

3. If you don't hurry, you will _____ your next class.

4. Iris wrapped the fragile teacup in tissue paper with _____.

5. We admired the forest for its natural _____.

6. Cheryl was absolutely _____ that she had won first place.

7. You would not _____ the news I just heard about the game!

8. Marcia's cat could _____ that the neighbor's dog was nearby.

LANGUAGE LINES

Parts of speech include nouns, pronouns, prepositions, adjectives, verbs, adverbs, and clauses.

Write the letter of the part of speech that matches the underlined word or words.

_____ 1. My family <u>traveled</u> to France last summer.

_____ 2. Adam was <u>very</u> pleased with his performance.

_____ 3. We brought <u>our</u> books to class.

_____ 4. Shelly <u>can</u> walk to the store from her house.

_____ 5. <u>I have a puppy</u> that I play with every day.

_____ 6. The fans <u>inside the gym</u> were cheering loudly.

_____ 7. <u>She</u> made the winning goal for her team.

_____ 8. Australia is the <u>smallest</u> continent.

a. personal pronoun

b. prepositional phrase

c. adjective

d. past tense verb

e. possessive pronoun

f. helping verb

g. independent clause

h. adverb

In My Own Words

What is the best gift that you have ever given someone? What made it so special?

Mind Jigglers

Say Cheese!

A. People say "cheese" when they have their photos taken because the **/ee/** sound makes their mouths widen into a smile. What are three other food words that would also do this?

1. _____   2. _____   3. _____

B. Use the clues to figure out the words. The letters in each word can all be found in the word *CAMERA*.

a male sheep: _____

the card before **2**: _____

a speed contest: _____

a female horse: _____

rich milk to whip: _____

means *arrived*: _____

to fill by force: _____

C. Carrie has arranged her photos in a display of 9 rows. The first row has 7 photos, the second has 6, the third has 7, the fourth has 6, and so on. How many photos are in Carrie's display?

_____ photos

Carrie is in every fourth photo. How many photos is Carrie in?

_____ photos

D. Michael traveled to Yellowstone National Park with his family. He had a camera, but he did not take any pictures. Give three possible reasons.

1. _____

2. _____

3. _____

E. Write a four-word sentence about taking a picture, usir

_____

MATH TIME

Riddle Me This

A. Study the table below to see which sports students like to watch on TV.

	Football	Basketball	Soccer	Baseball
Boys	10	4	11	3
Girls	5	9	12	1

Now use the information to draw a double bar graph below. Match the colors in the table to the colors on your graph.

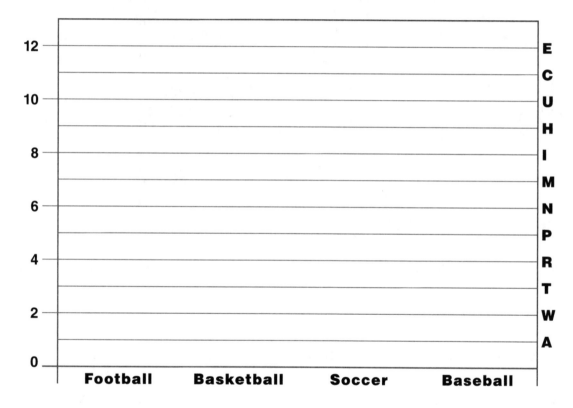

B. Each line below has a sport and a gender listed under it corresponding to one of the bars you drew on the graph. Look for the letter along the right that aligns with the top of each bar. Write that letter on the corresponding line to spell out the answer to this riddle:

What is bought by the yard and worn by the foot?

_____	_____	_____	_____	_____	_____
soccer	baseball	basketball	football	soccer	baseball
boys	girls	boys	girls	girls	boys

Geography

Northern Europe

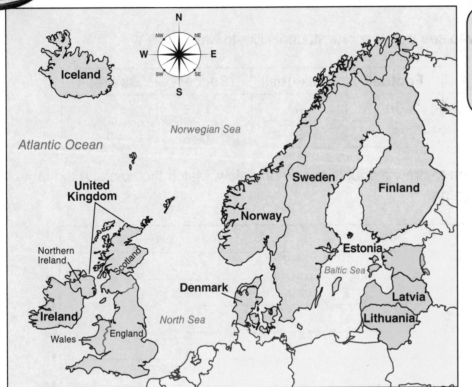

Key
Scandinavia: Purple
British Isles: Green
Baltic States: Pink

Use the map to answer the questions.

1. Which country is south of Latvia? _____

2. Which sea is west of Denmark? _____

3. Which country borders Sweden to the west? _____

4. Which country is Wales a part of? _____

5. Which island country is part of Scandinavia? _____

6. Which sea borders the Baltic states? _____

7. Which countries make up Scandinavia?

_____

WEEK 10

Check off each box as you complete the day's work.

Spelling Words

agency

cinnamon

contagious

cyclone

emergency

genetic

gymnasium

innocence

mythology

precise

rhinoceros

surgical

Get Creative!

What would your pencil say if it could talk?

A Memorable Moment

What sticks in your mind about this week? Write about it.

_____

_____

_____

_____

_____

_____

_____

Reading Record

	Book Title	Pages	Time
Monday	_____	_____	_____
Tuesday	_____	_____	_____
Wednesday	_____	_____	_____
Thursday	_____	_____	_____
Friday	_____	_____	_____

Describe a character you read about this week.

_____

_____

_____

_____

_____

_____

Read the story. Then answer the questions.

Three Parts for Three Characters

Denzel could hear the sounds of the song "Follow the Yellow Brick Road" as he walked closer to the auditorium. He was relieved that the auditions weren't over. He really wanted to try out for the sixth-grade production of *The Wizard of Oz*. Waiting in the hall were his two best friends, Colin and Felipe. Colin was walking on his hands in a wide circle. Then he did a cartwheel into a back handspring, finishing with a back flip. Felipe was doing his favorite herky-jerky robot dance.

Just as Denzel reached the boys, there was a sudden boom outside. "What was that?" Denzel shouted. He had a voice that could be loud and strong one moment and drop to a whisper the next instant.

"It's thunder," Colin laughed. "You should audition for the role of the character who needs courage!"

"Come on!" Felipe urged with a stiff bow to end his dance. "We'll miss our turns!"

The trio hurried inside the auditorium. A girl named Rachel, with hair teased like a lion's mane, was beginning her audition. The boys watched her. She pranced around the stage like a lion, but she spoke very quietly, and it was hard to hear her. When she finished, Felipe auditioned by dancing like a robot. Colin went next, showing his acrobatic skills. Denzel went last.

When the auditions ended, each boy had the perfect part for his talents. Colin was the Scarecrow, who is supposed to flop, slip, and slide all over the stage. Felipe's robot moves were just like the Tin Man in his rusty metal suit. And Denzel's booming roar and soft whisper made him the best Cowardly Lion the play could have.

. . . .

1. There is evidence in the passage to support the idea that Denzel _____.

   Ⓐ has never acted in a play before

   Ⓑ is always late

   Ⓒ is easily startled

   Ⓓ does not get along with Colin

2. What is the reason that Denzel got the part of the Cowardly Lion?

   Ⓐ It was the only part available.

   Ⓑ He was scared of the thunder.

   Ⓒ No one else auditioned for the part.

   Ⓓ He had the right voice for the role.

3. Why did Colin get the role of Scarecrow?

   Ⓐ He is good at doing acrobatics.

   Ⓑ He is a very serious person.

   Ⓒ He used dance moves during the audition.

   Ⓓ He had his hair teased for the part.

4. In the passage, which of these happens first?

   Ⓐ The boys get the perfect parts.

   Ⓑ Colin and Felipe practice in the hallway.

   Ⓒ Denzel hears a loud clap of thunder.

   Ⓓ A girl named Rachel finishes her audition.

Write It Right

Rewrite each sentence, correcting the errors.

1. Jacobs dad braught the tent from last years' camping trip but there was a tare in it

_____

_____

2. I eight alot of grape's pine apple chunks and water melon, at the picknick last Wenesday

_____

_____

3. We could'nt find no flours to pick for our Mother on Valintine's day.

_____

_____

MATH TIME

Round each number to complete the chart.

Number	Nearest Ten	Nearest Hundred	Nearest Thousand	Nearest Ten Thousand
76,242				
38,594				
98,399				
352,905				
990,376				
1,021,955				

© Evan-Moor Corp. • EMC 1068 • Daily Summer Activities

SPELL IT

When **c** comes before **e**, **i**, or **y**, it makes the soft /s/ sound.
When **g** comes before **e**, **i**, or **y**, it makes the soft /j/ sound.

Fill in the missing letter or letters to make the spelling words for the week. Then circle the letter or letters that make the **/s/** or **/j/** sound.

1. a_____cy

2. _____clone

3. _____gency

4. sur_____cal

5. conta_____

6. myth_____gy

7. _____nocer_____

8. inno_____

9. cin_____mon

10. _____cise

11. gen_____tic

12. gymna_____

In My Own Words

Pretend that you are just three inches tall for one day.
What would you do during your three-inch day?

LANGUAGE LINES

The **antecedent** of a pronoun is the noun (or nouns) to which it refers.

The antecedent does not have to be in the same sentence as the pronoun.

The **rider** rode to the next station. There, a fresh horse was waiting for **him**.
(antecedent)   (pronoun)

Circle each pronoun. Then draw an arrow from the pronoun to its antecedent.

1. The Pony Express helped unify a nation. It was very successful.

2. About 180 riders took part. They were on the trail day and night.

3. The riders traveled in any weather, no matter how bad it got.

4. Mail was delivered in 10 days during the summer months. It took two weeks in the winter.

5. Many people depended on the Pony Express, and they were thankful for its services.

6. A rider for the Pony Express had to be an expert. He also had to be willing to risk death.

MATH TIME

Solve the word problems.

Skyler took a lot of photos on his Grand Canyon trip. He deleted one-third of them. Then he uploaded half of the remaining photos to a photo-managing site. He ordered prints of one-fourth of the uploaded photos and gave half of the prints away. The number of prints he gave away was 24. How many photos did Skyler originally take?

_____ photos

Skyler's little sister Jasmine took a lot of photos, too. She took 354 photos altogether: 286 were of scenery, and 128 were of people. How many were of both scenery and people?

_____ photos

Jasmine put 25% of the photos of people in an album. How many photos did she put in the album?

_____ photos

Read the article. Then answer the questions.

The World in a Pond

An ecosystem is a community of living and nonliving things that work together. Organisms, light, heat, soil, water, and the atmosphere are all parts of an ecosystem. Any alteration to an ecosystem—such as changes in temperature, the kinds of animals living there, or pollution—can affect all parts of it. This can be especially obvious in the small, enclosed ecosystem of a pond.

In a pond, sunlight helps tiny plants called *algae* grow. Algae release oxygen, which fish need in order to breathe. Algae are also food for other tiny organisms, which are in turn eaten by fish. The fish then give off carbon dioxide, which plants use to grow.

Imagine what would happen, however, if certain conditions changed in the pond. For example, if sunlight didn't reach the pond because of thick pollution, or if the temperature of the water grew colder or warmer, the algae wouldn't grow. Without algae, there would first be less oxygen. Tiny organisms would starve. Fish would die from the lack of oxygen. Plants would then die without the carbon dioxide that fish give off. And larger animals that eat the plants and smaller animals would not get enough food. Even humans, who eat the plants, fish, and larger animals, would feel the impact. The whole ecosystem would suffer.

. . . .

1. **Which of these would happen first if algae stopped growing in a pond?**

   Ⓐ Fish would die.

   Ⓑ There would be less carbon dioxide.

   Ⓒ There would be less oxygen.

   Ⓓ Plants would die.

2. **After the tiny organisms that eat algae died, the next thing to happen would be that _____.**

   Ⓐ the fish would die

   Ⓑ plants would lack carbon dioxide

   Ⓒ humans would go hungry

   Ⓓ larger animals would have less food

3. **Plants would die in a pond after _____.**

   Ⓐ the amount of oxygen decreased

   Ⓑ humans were affected

   Ⓒ larger animals went hungry

   Ⓓ the amount of carbon dioxide decreased

4. **Which of these would be the last to feel the effects of a lack of algae?**

   Ⓐ fish

   Ⓑ plants

   Ⓒ humans

   Ⓓ tiny organisms

Vo·cab·u·lar·y

Homographs are words that are spelled the same but have different meanings. They can also be different parts of speech.

Identify the part of speech for the bold word in each sentence and write it on the fist line. Then, on the second line, write another sentence using the *homograph* of the bold word. Use the definitions in the box to help you.

sage	*n.*	an herb	**flounder**	*n.*	a marine flatfish
	adj.	wise		*v.*	to struggle clumsily
loom	*n.*	a frame for weaving	**spell**	*n.*	a magical charm
	v.	to appear in front of, looking big or scary		*v.*	to give the letters of a word in order
reel	*n.*	a device for winding string			
	v.	to stagger or whirl			

1. Report cards **loom** on the schedule just before winter break. _____

   _____

2. After fishing all day, we had **flounder** for dinner. _____

   _____

3. The guidance counselor offered **sage** advice on applying to colleges. _____

   _____

4. I wish I knew a **spell** for growing tall. _____

   _____

5. An hour of math homework is enough to make my brain **reel**. _____

   _____

LANGUAGE LINES

A phrase that is necessary to the meaning of a sentence is called a **restrictive phrase**.
A phrase that is *not* necessary to the meaning of a sentence is called a **nonrestrictive phrase**.
A nonrestrictive phrase is separated from the rest of the sentence by commas.

Write *R* for *restrictive* or *NR* for *nonrestrictive* above the underlined clauses, and add commas if needed.

1. Students <u>who finish their assignments early</u> don't have to take the test.

2. Jack and Linda <u>who live on a boat</u> have traveled all over the world.

3. The wind <u>which was strong and cold</u> blew the clothes off the line.

4. Climates <u>that have both cold and warm weather</u> are called "temperate."

5. San Pablo <u>where Marta was born</u> is a small town in Argentina.

In My Own Words

Describe an event that changed your life.

© Evan-Moor Corp. • EMC 1068 • Daily Summer Activities

Mind Jigglers

Glue and Tape

Twelve compound words got cut in half. Your job is to "tape" them back together. Write a compound word in each box at the bottom of the page. But be careful— you may use each word only once.

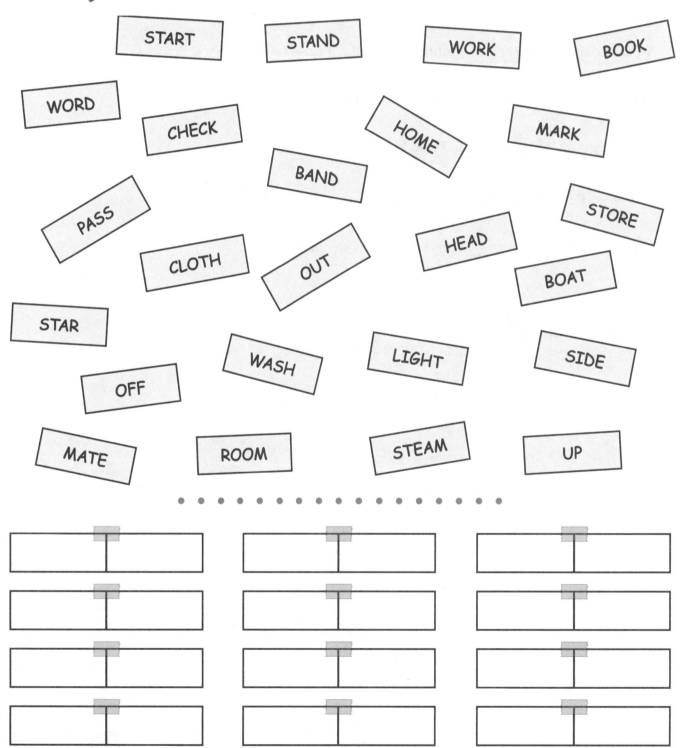

START   STAND   WORK   BOOK

WORD   CHECK   HOME   MARK

BAND

PASS   STORE

CLOTH   OUT   HEAD   BOAT

STAR

WASH   LIGHT   SIDE

OFF

MATE   ROOM   STEAM   UP

MATH TIME

Trapezoids

The formula for finding the area of a trapezoid:

$$A = \tfrac{1}{2} \times (b_1 + b_2) \times h$$

This formula means that you add the lengths of the two bases and multiply that sum by $\tfrac{1}{2}$. Then multiply that product by the height.

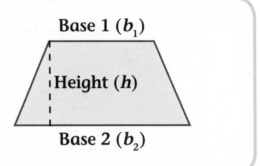

Base 1 (b_1)

Height (h)

Base 2 (b_2)

Use the formula to find the area of each trapezoid below.

1.
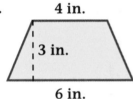
4 in.

3 in.

6 in.

A = _____

2.
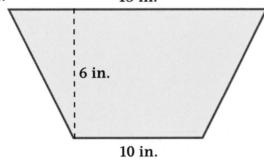
15 in.

6 in.

10 in.

A = _____

3.
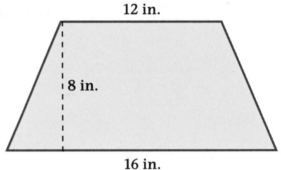
12 in.

8 in.

16 in.

A = _____

4.
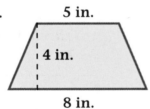
5 in.

4 in.

8 in.

A = _____

Southwest Asia (Middle East)

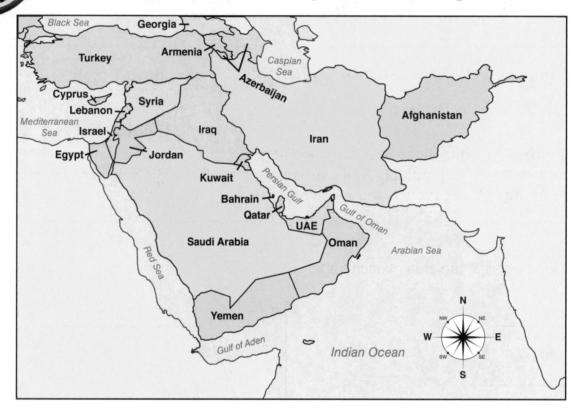

Use the map to answer the questions.

1. Which country borders Iran to the east? _____

2. Which sea borders Syria? _____

3. Which country has the longest border along the Red Sea? _____

4. How many countries border Israel? List them.

_____

5. How many countries border Iraq? List them.

_____

Answer Key

Checking your child's work is an important part of learning. It allows you to see what your child knows well and what areas need more practice. It also provides an opportunity for you to help your child understand that making mistakes is a part of learning.

The answer key pages can be used in several ways:

➤ Remove the answer pages and give the book to your child. Go over the answers with him or her as each day's work is completed.

➤ Leave the answer pages in the book and give the practice pages to your child one day at a time.

➤ Leave the answer pages in the book so your child can check his or her own work as the pages are completed. It is still important to review the pages with your child if you use this method.

Week 1 — Page 11

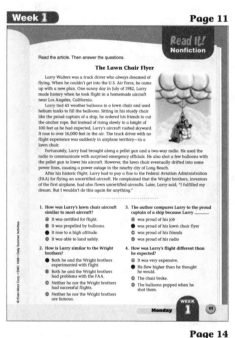

Read It! Nonfiction — The Lawn Chair Flyer

1. Ⓐ It rose to a high altitude.
2. Both he and the Wright brothers had problems with the F.A.A.
3. was proud of his lawn chair flyer
4. He flew higher than he thought he would.

Page 12 — Write It Right

1. My neighbor gave me two homemade chocolate chip cookies.
2. Did you know that tomorrow is my dad's birthday?
3. My sister and I have a white dog named Skippy.
4. My aunt opened an antique shop on Liberty Street last week.

MATH TIME

Solve the percentage problems.

1. What is 40% of each number?
   5 → 2   80 → 32
   95 → 38   110 → 44

2. What is 75% of each number?
   8 → 6   24 → 18
   68 → 51   200 → 150

3. What is 23% of each number?
   6 → 1.38   123 → 28.29
   35 → 8.05   76 → 17.48

4. What is 7% of each number?
   3 → 0.21   177 → 12.39
   65 → 4.55   234 → 16.38

Page 13 — SPELL IT

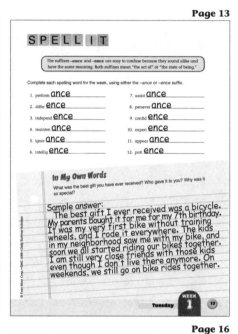

1. perform — ance
2. differ — ence
3. independ — ence
4. mainten — ance
5. ignor — ance
6. intellig — ence
7. assist — ance
8. persever — ance
9. confid — ence
10. experi — ence
11. appear — ance
12. pati — ence

In My Own Words

Sample answer:
The best gift I ever received was a bicycle. My parents bought it for me for my 7th birthday. It was my very first bike without training wheels, and I rode it everywhere. The kids in my neighborhood saw me with my bike, and soon we all started riding our bikes together. I am still very close friends with those kids even though I don't live there anymore. On weekends, we still go on bike rides together.

Page 14 — LANGUAGE LINES

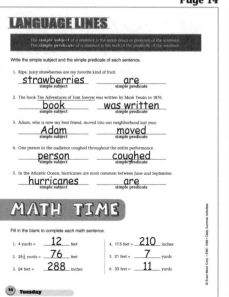

Write the simple subject and the simple predicate of each sentence.

1. strawberries / are
2. book / was written
3. Adam / moved
4. person / coughed
5. hurricanes / are

MATH TIME

Fill in the blank to complete each math sentence.

1. 4 yards = 12 feet
2. 25⅓ yards = 76 feet
3. 24 feet = 288 inches
4. 17.5 feet = 210 inches
5. 21 feet = 7 yards
6. 33 feet = 11 yards

Page 15 — Read It! Nonfiction

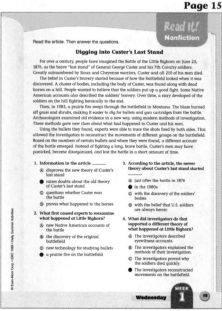

Digging into Custer's Last Stand

1. raises doubts about the old theory of Custer's last stand
2. a prairie fire on the battlefield
3. in the 1980s
4. The investigators reconstructed movements on the battlefield.

Page 16 — Vocabulary

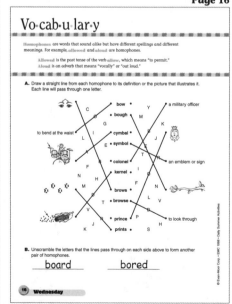

A. Draw a straight line from each homophone to its definition or the picture that illustrates it.

B. Unscramble the letters that the lines pass through on each side above to form another pair of homophones.

board   bored

LANGUAGE LINES

Compound sentences are made by joining two or more simple sentences containing related information. They are formed using a comma and a coordinating conjunction.

Form a compound sentence by joining the simple sentences with a comma and the coordinating conjunction *or*, *and*, or *but*.

1. I looked for my homework on my desk. I forgot to look on the kitchen table.

I looked for my homework on my desk, but I forgot to look on the kitchen table.

2. Maybe I left it on the bus. Maybe I left it in the cafeteria.

Maybe I left it on the bus, or maybe I left it in the cafeteria.

3. I went into my bedroom. I found it under the bed.

I went into my bedroom, and I found it under the bed.

In My Own Words

What has been the high point of your day so far? What has been the low point?

Sample answer:
The high point of my day was waking up to the smell of breakfast cooking in the kitchen. Mom made pancakes, eggs, potatoes, and bacon, and it was delicious. The low point was seeing dark clouds roll in, which meant a thunderstorm was on its way. I was planning on going swimming in the lake today, but now it looks like I will have to stay home.

Thursday WEEK 1 17

Mind Jigglers

Favorite Animals

Match each person with his or her favorite animal in the box. Read the clues in the chart to find the answers. Each animal may be used only once.

bear cub	chipmunk	hamster	monkey	puppy
calf	dolphin	kitten	mouse	rabbit
canary	fawn	ladybug	penguin	raccoon
chick	frog	lamb	piglet	squirrel

Name	Clue	Animal
Mara	is usually white	lamb
Anthony	is a bird	penguin
Fiona	lives in the jungle	monkey
Laura	is an insect	ladybug
Daphne	has long ears	rabbit
Katie	contains four of the letters that are in her name	kitten
Jake	lives in a cage	canary
Derek	was found at a pond	frog
Andy	ends with the same letter as his name	puppy
Drew	begins with the same letter as his name	dolphin
Peter	contains the same number of letters as his name	mouse
Lucy	is the third-smallest pet	hamster
Shari	is a baby animal	bear cub
Annie	contains two pairs of double letters	raccoon
Kevin	is not a mammal	chick
Miranda	lives on a farm	piglet
Chad	contains the same number of letters as his name	fawn or calf
Joey	stores nuts	squirrel
Luke	contains the same number of letters as his name	calf or fawn
Carl	begins with the same letter as his name	chipmunk

18 **Thursday**

MATH TIME

Plotting Coordinates

Plot the ordered pairs of numbers in the order in which they are listed. Then connect the points with straight lines. Start each new set of points with a new line.

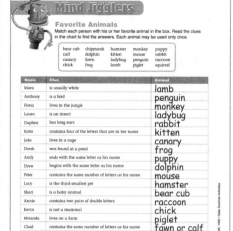

Coordinates

▶ **Set 1:** (−2, −10) (−1, −10) (−1, −9) (1, −9) (1, −10) (2, −10) (2, −7) (1, −7) (1, −8) (−1, −8) (−1, −7) (−2, −7) (−2, −10)

▶ **Set 2:** (−7, −11) (7, −7) (6, −2) (5, 0) (4, −2) (3, −4) (1, −6) (−1, −6) (−3, −4) (−4, −2) (−5, 0) (−6, −2) (−7, −7) (−7, −11)

▶ **Set 3:** (−1, −4) (1, −4) (1, −2) (−1, −2) (−1, −4)

▶ **Set 4:** (2, 2) (3, 3) (4, 3) (4, 2) (2, 2)

▶ **Set 5:** (−2, 2) (−2, 3) (−4, 3) (−4, 2) (−2, 2)

▶ **Set 6:** (5, 0) (6, 6) (7, 2) (8, 1) (9, 1) (10, 2) (10, 7) (9, 7) (10, 3) (11, 3) (11, 7) (10, 10) (−9, 9) (−10, 7) (−10, 2) (−9, 1) (−8, 1) (−7, 2) (−6, 6) (−5, 0)

Friday WEEK 1 19

Geography

Australia and Oceania

[map of Australia and Oceania]

Legend
- Mountains
- Desert
- Great Barrier Reef
- Mountain Peak

Use the map to answer the questions.

1. In which country are the Southern Alps located?

New Zealand

2. Which Australian desert is farthest south?

Great Victoria

3. What is the name of the mountain peak in Papua New Guinea?

Mount Wilhelm

4. Which landform is located in the sea just off the northeastern coast of Australia?

Great Barrier Reef

5. Which Australian desert is farthest east?

Simpson

6. What is the name of the mountain peak in Australia?

Mount Kosciuszko

20 **Friday**

Read It! Fiction

Read the story. Then answer the questions.

The Elephant and the Hummingbird

Long, long ago—in the days when people could talk to animals and learn their stories—an elephant walked slowly beside the Yellow River. This was before animals were tamed, even before the first Chinese emperors ruled. That's how long ago it was.

The elephant was enjoying a peaceful stroll. Thick grasses and beautiful lotus flowers bloomed, and the water in the Yellow River made a pleasant swishing sound as it flowed past the elephant.

Noticing what appeared to be a hummingbird, the elephant stopped. The elephant had seen hummingbirds before. He'd watched them hover above lotus flowers, their wings beating so quickly that they appeared only as a blur. The elephant sometimes wished he could move as quickly as a hummingbird. This one, however, was lying upside down, her wings motionless and her legs pointing toward the sky. Occasionally, the little bird would sigh heavily or grunt, as if working extra hard.

"What are you doing?" asked the elephant. He slowly walked around the hummingbird, trying to understand the odd behavior. "You look ridiculous, you know."

"I am holding up the sky," replied the hummingbird calmly. "I overheard that it might fall today."

The elephant raised his trunk and bellowed a deep, loud laugh. "You're holding up the sky? Why, just look at it. The sky is bigger than I am, and I doubt you could hold me up. Even if the sky were going to fall, your tiny legs could not possibly do the job."

"Ah," said the hummingbird, "but these are the only legs I have. I might not be able to do it by myself, but I am doing what I can."

1. Where and when does the folk tale take place?
ⓐ on a ship on the Yellow River
ⓑ on a bridge around AD 1400
ⓒ in a Chinese flower garden
● beside a river in ancient China

2. How does the elephant probably feel about what the hummingbird is doing?
ⓐ He thinks she is smart.
ⓑ He thinks she is arrogant.
● He thinks she is wasting her time.
ⓓ He thinks she is selfish.

3. What is the message of the folk tale?
● People should do what they can with what they have.
ⓑ Past wisdom is better than present wisdom.
ⓒ It is always best not to look ridiculous.
ⓓ It is risky to try things that other people say are impossible.

4. Which of these conflicts is important in the story?
ⓐ good vs. evil
ⓑ trying vs. watching
ⓒ strength vs. weakness
ⓓ being tame vs. being free

Monday WEEK 2 23

Write It Right

Rewrite each sentence, correcting the errors.

1. only kids who has past the swimming test are aloud to swim in the deap end of the pool

Only kids who have passed the swimming test are allowed to swim in the deep end of the pool.

2. at the zoo we saw a lion a elefant and a giraffe

At the zoo we saw a lion, an elephant, and a giraffe.

3. maria always eats three shugar cookie's after dinner

Maria always eats three sugar cookies after dinner.

MATH TIME

Complete the function tables using the given rule. The first entry has been done for you.

1.
Rule: × 3 − 12	
Input	Output
12	24
8	12
5	3
3	−3

2.
Rule: ÷ 3 × 11	
Input	Output
2	55
4	77
9	132
15	198

3.
Rule: × 3 − 5	
Input	Output
19	52
15	40
8	19
1	−2

4.
Rule: × 5 + 1	
Input	Output
3	16
4	21
8	41
10	51

24 **Monday**

SPELL IT

Words are usually divided into syllables between double consonants, after a consonant that follows a short vowel, or after a long vowel.

lit|tle   pen|cil   pa|per

Write the spelling words for the words. Then draw lines to divide each word into syllables. Use a dictionary to help you.

1. ac|com|plish
2. as|so|ci|ate
3. broc|co|li
4. com|mer|cial
5. flam|ma|ble
6. hip|po|pot|a|mus
7. mes|sen|ger
8. pos|sess
9. scis|sors
10. suc|ceed
11. sum|ma|ry
12. vac|ci|nate

In My Own Words

Your parents have decided that your new bedtime is 8:00 PM! What can you say to convince them that this is a bad idea?

Sample answer:
Mom and Dad, if you change my bedtime to 8:00, I will barely have enough time to finish my homework and eat dinner! After soccer practice, I come home and start doing my homework. Then we eat at 6:00, and I finish my homework after dinner. If eating together as a family is important to you, then you need to let me stay up later. Also, I should be able to enjoy a little downtime. After all, I am still a kid. I should be able to have fun, too!

Tuesday WEEK 2 25

LANGUAGE LINES

A verb phrase is made up of a helping verb and a main verb. Helping verbs include:
am is are was were has can should could must will

Write the helping verb and the main verb in the correct columns.

	Helping Verb	Main Verb
1. My town has built a new playing field.	has	built
2. The football team can play on Friday nights now.	can	play
3. You must come to our next game.	must	come
4. We are improving every week.	are	improving
5. By the next game, we should be great!	should	be
6. I know we will win our next game.	will	win

MATH TIME

The Galloway family recorded the amount of money they collected at their garage sale in the chart below. Use the chart to answer the questions.

Person	Money Collected
Ginny	45¢, $1.75, 75¢, $1.25
Justin	$2.00, $2.00, $1.50, 25¢
Lucas	$3.00, $1.75, 30¢
Lia	90¢, 35¢, 25¢, 10¢, 75¢

1. How much money did each family member make at the yard sale?

Ginny: $4.20   Lucas: $5.05
Justin: $5.75   Lia: $2.35

2. How much money did the family make altogether? $17.35

26 **Tuesday**

Read It! Fiction

Read the story. Then answer the questions.

Up to the Mountaintop

I like challenges, but this one was almost too difficult. I had begged Mom to take me on a completely new adventure for my sixteenth birthday. Now, here we were, just Mom and me with our guide, Milo, standing on the shore of Lake Arenal in Costa Rica. Towering above the lake was Volcán Arenal, one of the active volcanoes in the region. I watched as the volcano spit up lava and coughed up big boulders. Luckily, we were headed in the other direction.

Milo helped us mount our horses. Getting on my horse was difficult, but controlling it was a little easier. We started on our ride. The guidebook said we'd cross three rivers. As we splashed through a gentle stream, I asked hopefully, "Is this the first river?"

"I don't think so, Katie," Mom said wryly.

Soon enough, we came to a *real* river. There was no mistaking it. I felt sick to my stomach when I saw that the far shore was half a football field away! The four-foot-deep river flowed over large boulders. So much for dry shoes—or jeans.

After two more rivers, the trail got steeper and muddier. With each step of the horses' hooves, there were lou[d]... absolutely beautiful. [...] mud. What did I kno[...] beneath the sludge[...]

Three treacherous[...] To one side was a go[...] painted restaurant. "[...]

1. Which adjective[...]
ⓐ sensitive and[...]
ⓑ calm and rel[...]
● adventurous[...]
ⓓ interested bu[...]

2. Which inference[...] Katie's experie[...]
ⓐ She is an ex[...]
ⓑ She has pro[...] to ride.
ⓒ She dislikes[...]
ⓓ She has litt[...] horses.

Wednesday WEEK 2 27

province — division of certain countries
synonym — territory, region

Daily Summer Activities

© Ev[...]

Answer Key

Vo·cab·u·lar·y

A **prefix** is a word part that comes at the beginning of a word and affects its meaning. Knowing the meanings of prefixes can sometimes help you figure out the meanings of words.

The prefixes *mega–*, *magni–*, and *macro–* mean "large" or "great."
The prefixes *micro–* and *mini–* mean "small."

Write *mega–*, *magni–*, *macro–*, *micro–*, or *mini–* to form words that will make sense in each sentence below. Then write the words to complete the sentences.

magnify	**magni**tude	**macro**biotic	**mini**mum	**mini**ature
megalith	**macro**cosm	**mega**phone /**micro**	**micro**phone /**mega**	**micro**scope

1. Coach Flexman uses a __megaphone__ to project his voice across the field.
2. Ancient people moved the giant __megalith__ without machines.
3. I saw tiny hairs on the fly's legs when I looked at it under a __microscope__.
4. The optometrist uses a lens to __magnify__ images to 10 times their size.
5. Nick thinks a __macrobiotic__ diet will help him live to 100 years old.
6. I love astronomy, so I want to study the entire __macrocosm__.
7. The Richter scale is used to measure the __magnitude__ of earthquakes.
8. In order to amplify her voice, the jazz singer needed a __microphone__.
9. We bought __miniature__ furniture for my sister's dollhouse.
10. The __minimum__ speed limit on the interstate is 45 miles per hour.

28 Wednesday

LANGUAGE LINES

A **compound subject** contains two or more simple subjects that are joined by a coordinating conjunction and share the same verb. A **compound predicate** tells two or more things about the same subject, without repeating the subject.

Write *compound subject* or *compound predicate* after each sentence. The first one has been done for you.

1. I did my math homework and wrote my essay. — compound predicate
2. Wendy lives in Holland and speaks Dutch. — compound predicate
3. Carrie, Emily, and Jack went to the movies. — compound subject
4. Andrew ate a hot dog and scarfed down a hamburger. — compound predicate
5. Mr. and Mrs. Benefit announced their new baby boy. — compound subject
6. Meghan watched her dog take off and chased after him — compound predicate

In My Own Words

Imagine you are a novelist working on your next mystery. Describe your main character. What is his or her name? What does he or she look like? Name at least two personality traits of your character.

Sample answer:
In my next mystery novel, my main character's name will be Henry Hasselbury. Henry is a widowed older man in his 70s. He is tall and slim with bright blue eyes and a friendly grin. He was always a shy but sweet man, but in the years since his wife died, he has become more and more distant. Now he has trouble even leaving his own home. He just wants to be invisible.

Thursday 2 29

Mind Jigglers
Clocks and Calendars

A. Complete the time-related phrases. Example: 12 months in a year

60 s**econds** in a m**inute**
100 y**ears** in a c**entury**
24 h**ours** in a d**ay**
52 w**eeks** in a y**ear**
60 m**inutes** in an h**our**
365 d**ays** in a y**ear**
31 d**ays** in a m**onth**
10 y**ears** in a d**ecade**
72 h**ours** in 3 d**ays**
120 m**inutes** in 2 h**ours**
24 m**onths** in 2 y**ears**

B. Solve the time-related riddles.
Carrie practices piano from 3:10 until 3:55 PM. How long does she practice?
__45__ minutes

Miranda babysat her brother for 3 hours and 45 minutes. She started at 11:30 AM. At what time did she finish?
3:15 PM

It took Samantha 47 minutes to do her homework. She finished at 8:22 PM. When did she start?
7:35 PM

Charlotte dances ballet for 2.5 hours twice each week. How many hours will she have danced in 12 weeks?
__60__ hours

C. Guess the phrase. Look at the way the words are written, including word order and placement, to find the answer.

TimeTime	DAY'S all WORK	S E M I T
time after time	all in a day's work	time's up

30 Thursday

MATH TIME
Measuring Angles

Measure each of the angles in the orange box with a protractor (to the nearest 5°). Then write the corresponding letter above the angle measurement below the box. The letters will spell out the answer to the riddle.

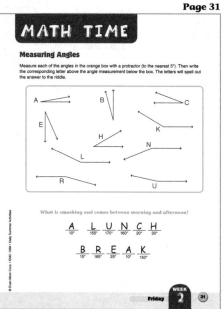

What is smashing and comes between morning and afternoon?

A L U N C H
10° 155° 170° 160° 20° 30°

B R E A K
15° 165° 25° 10° 150°

Friday 2 31

Geography
Canada and Greenland

The country of Canada is divided into ten provinces and three territories. The territories are in the north, and the provinces are in the south.

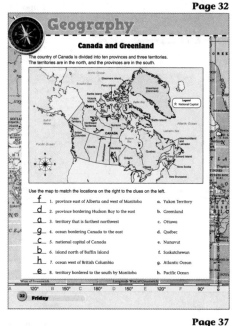

Use the map to match the locations on the right to the clues on the left.

f 1. province east of Alberta and west of Manitoba — a. Yukon Territory
a 2. province bordering Hudson Bay to the east — b. Greenland
d 3. territory that is farthest northwest — c. Ottawa
g 4. ocean bordering Canada to the east — d. Québec
c 5. national capital of Canada — e. Nunavut
b 6. island north of Baffin Island — f. Saskatchewan
h 7. ocean west of British Columbia — g. Atlantic Ocean
e 8. territory bordered to the south by Manitoba — h. Pacific Ocean

A 120° B 150° C 180° D 150° E 120° F 90°

32 Friday

Read It!
Nonfiction

Read the article. Then answer the questions.

Tall Tale Heroes

Life for American pioneers was hard, and their work was often tedious. For entertainment, they told funny stories called "tall tales." The stories had larger-than-life characters and were filled with exaggerations. Two famous tall tale characters were Paul Bunyan and Pecos Bill.

Imagine a giant lumberjack who could topple an acre of trees with one hand. That was Paul Bunyan. Bunyan was so big that he had to eat 40 bowls of porridge just to whet his appetite. His faithful companion was an immense blue ox named Babe. Their rain-filled footprints became the 10,000 lakes of Minnesota. According to stories, surviving in the North Woods was an achievement. One winter, it was so cold that Babe's milk turned straight to ice cream!

Do you know of any cowboy who would ride a horse named Widowmaker? That was Pecos Bill, who also galloped around on a mountain lion. Legend says that Bill fell from his parents' wagon when he was a baby. Coyotes rescued Bill and raised him in the wild. He could rope a whole herd of cattle at once, or even lasso a cyclone. And when he anticipated trouble, he carried a live rattlesnake as a whip. Bill's girlfriend was also famous for her frequent stunts. Sluefoot Sue once took a pleasant ride on a giant catfish down the Rio Grande River!

Paul Bunyan and Pecos Bill are just two examples of the imaginative characters who represented the hope and spirit of America's pioneers. Their stories still entertain us today.

1. A tall tale is filled with
   Ⓐ historical events
   Ⓑ mysteries and magic
   ● exaggerations and humor
   Ⓓ sad stories

2. Which words describe Babe, the blue ox?
   Ⓐ slow, cranky
   ● immense, faithful
   Ⓒ tall, lazy
   Ⓓ watchful, mean

3. Who is not a character in a tall tale?
   Ⓐ Pecos Bill
   Ⓑ Sluefoot Sue
   ● Harry Potter
   Ⓓ Paul Bunyan

4. According to stories, one winter it was so cold that...
   Ⓐ birds flew backwards.
   Ⓑ tulips bloomed in December.
   Ⓒ hens laid hard-boiled eggs.
   ● milk turned straight to ice cream.

Monday 3 35

Write It Right

Rewrite each sentence, correcting the errors.

1. woud you like to eat a apple or a bananna?
   Would you like to eat an apple or a banana?

2. in the united, states we celebrate independence day on july forth.
   In the United States, we celebrate Independence Day on July fourth.

3. make shure that you dont let your ice cream melt in the son.
   Make sure that you don't let your ice cream melt in the sun.

MATH TIME

Complete the table so that each row shows three representations of the same value. The first row has been done for you.

Fraction	Decimal	Percent
$\frac{7}{10}$	0.7	70%
$\frac{3}{10}$	0.3	30%
$\frac{3}{4}$	0.75	75%
$\frac{9}{10}$	0.9	90%
$\frac{3}{8}$	0.375	37.5%

36 Monday

SPELL IT

The suffix **–ous** often means "full of."

Write the spelling words for the week to match the clues below. Then underline the suffix in each word.

1. full of a need to find out: __curious__
2. full of ambition: __ambitious__
3. causing outrage: __outrageous__
4. causing great damage: __disastrous__
5. full of beauty: __gorgeous__
6. unidentified: __anonymous__
7. full of fierceness: __ferocious__
8. full of suspicion: __suspicious__
9. full of adventure: __adventurous__
10. full of courage: __courageous__
11. full of grace: __gracious__
12. full of politeness: __courteous__

In My Own Words

Describe either the oldest or the youngest person you know. Include as many details as you can.

Sample answer:
The youngest person I know is my baby cousin Amelia. She is only five months old. She has big, dark eyes, chubby cheeks, and soft brown hair. When she smiles, you can see the dimples in her cheeks. Amelia doesn't walk or even crawl yet, but she can sit up on her own and she can laugh.

Tuesday 3 37

LANGUAGE LINES

A **preposition** shows the relationship of a noun or pronoun to another word in the sentence. Words such as *above*, *behind*, *during*, *with*, and *for* are examples of prepositions.

Circle the preposition or prepositions in each sentence.

1. Katie hid behind the big oak tree.
2. Tom fell asleep during the movie.
3. Sanjay made a birthday card for his sister.
4. James stretched his arms above his head.
5. Carlos looked in his pocket for his keys.
6. Tim eats his dinner with chopsticks.
7. Jen ran into a tree during a game of tag.
8. Maria went with her mother to the store.
9. Chris ran around the house in bare feet.
10. Ben crawled under the fence carefully.

MATH TIME

Solve the measurement problems below.

1. Find the perimeter of the football field in feet. — 1,040 feet
2. Find the area of the football field in feet. — 57,600 feet
3. How many feet away from the end zone is the 50-yard line? — 150 feet

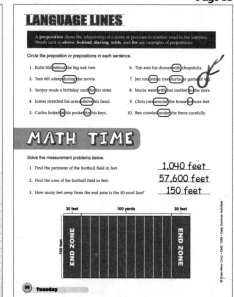

30 feet	100 yards	30 feet
END ZONE		END ZONE

36 Tuesday

3.75/1000

GCD is 125

Page 39

Read It! Fiction

Read the story. Then answer the questions.

A Diagnosis

Every Sunday at exactly 11:00 AM, my whole family gathers in the lobby of the Oak Valley Manor for Senior Citizens. That's when my parents, my brother Phillip, and I join my great-grandmother June for Sunday brunch—a spectacular buffet of omelets, pancakes, and French toast. Great-Grandma June's friend, Dr. Shepard, always joins us.

Lately, though, there has been a change in Dr. Shepard, who also lives at the Manor. When I first met him, he used a walker to get around but still stood straight and tall and always smiled. Now he seemed to move more slowly, hunched over his walker, and rarely smiled.

Recently, our dog Sally had been tired and hadn't wanted to play. Since pets are allowed in the Manor on Sundays, we decided to bring Sally along. As we walked in, we heard Dr. Shepard holler, "Come, Sally!" He reached out his arms and Sally ran to him, her tail wagging wildly. He scratched behind Sally's ears and gently rubbed her belly.

"Dogs are wonderful!" he said. "And I should know. I used to be a vet."

"Wow, you were a vet? Maybe you can figure out what's wrong with Sally," I said.

Dr. Shepard chuckled. "Maybe I can!" And with a huge smile he added, "Go ahead and join your family. I'll stay right here with Sally and see if I can make a diagnosis."

1. **What change does the narrator notice about Dr. Shepard before Dr. Shepard sees Sally?**
   - Ⓐ Dr. Shepard no longer joins the family for brunch.
   - ● Dr. Shepard moves more slowly and smiles less often.
   - Ⓒ Dr. Shepard is healthier and happier.
   - Ⓓ Dr. Shepard is no longer friends with Great-Grandma June.
2. **What is the main idea of the passage?**
   - Ⓐ A family brings their dog Sally to see a vet.
   - Ⓑ The Manor has a great buffet every Sunday.
   - ● Sally and Dr. Shepard are not feeling well but may be able to help each other.
   - Ⓓ The family visits Great-Grandma June at Oak Valley Manor.
3. **Which detail from the passage tells you that something is wrong with Sally?**
   - ● Sally is tired.
   - Ⓑ Sally runs to Dr. Shepard.
   - Ⓒ Sally wags her tail wildly.
   - Ⓓ Sally visits the Manor.
4. **What does the family normally do at Oak Valley Manor?**
   - Ⓐ They take Sally to see Dr. Shepard.
   - ● They eat brunch with Great-Grandma June.
   - Ⓒ They spend the morning with Sally.
   - Ⓓ They pick up Great-Grandma June for a day out.

Wednesday WEEK 3 39

Page 40

Vo·cab·u·lar·y

Antonyms are words that have opposite meanings.

Doubt is the opposite of certainty. Knowledge is the opposite of ignorance.

Every word in the grid below is an antonym of another word in the grid. Start with any word and draw a line to its antonym by passing through the empty squares. But you must move only vertically or horizontally, not diagonally, and none of your lines can cross. Use a pencil so you can erase. One line is drawn for you.

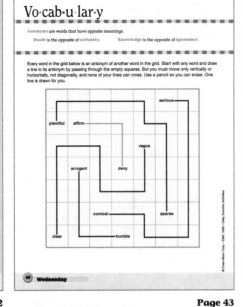

40 Wednesday

Page 41

LANGUAGE LINES

Irregular verbs have special past tense forms. For example, the past tense of **sing** is **sang**.

Write the correct past tense form of the verb in parentheses to complete each sentence.

1. We brought fresh-baked cookies to the picnic. **(bring)**
2. Emily chose three new shirts to buy at the store. **(choose)**
3. John watched as the sun slowly sank below the horizon. **(sink)**
4. Jeremy and Anna built a sand castle together. **(build)**
5. Katie couldn't go to the movies because she caught a cold. **(catch)**
6. Mrs. Collins told you not to pick those flowers. **(tell)**
7. My sister and I crept up slowly to the sleeping kitten. **(creep)**
8. I read the book from cover to cover. **(read)**
9. The doctor sought a cure for the deadly disease. **(seek)**
10. Smoke billowed into the air as the fire swept across the prairie. **(sweep)**

In My Own Words

If you could be any animal for one day, what animal would you be? What would you do on that day?

Sample answer:
If I could be an animal for a day, I would be a dolphin. I would swim in tropical waters and check out all the beautiful fish along the coral reefs. I would launch myself out of the water and do flips in the air. I would swim and play with my fellow dolphins all day.

Thursday WEEK 3 41

Page 42

Mind Jigglers

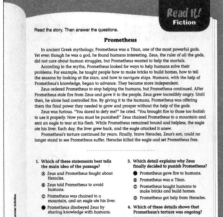

Arachnids

A. The answer is **a big black spider**. Write three different questions. They can be funny or serious. Sample answers:

1. What is dark, hairy, and has eight legs?
2. What kind of pet is best not to cuddle with?
3. What traps its food in a large web?

B. Unscramble the names of places where most people would not want to find a spider.

- RIHA hair
- HEOS shoe
- DEB bed
- DOSA soda
- WHACSIND sandwich
- CCAAKKPB backpack
- PUSO soup
- STANP pants

C. Draw a path that shows how the spider can get to all 10 flies and back to the center of the web without crossing its own path.

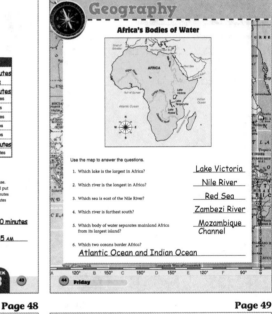

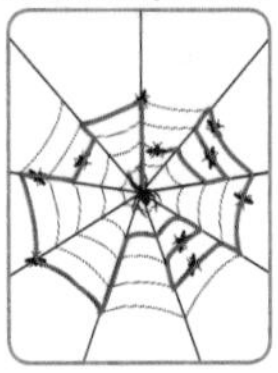

D. Finish the tongue twisters. Sample answers:

1. Sally the Spider saw Suzie swinging while singing softly.
2. Terry Tarantula tied thread to twenty-three twigs.

42 Thursday

Page 43

MATH TIME

Elapsed Time

A. Complete the chart by filling in all the empty spaces.

Starting Time	Ending Time	Elapsed Time
7:15 AM	9:00 AM	1 hour, 45 minutes
5:20 PM	6:15 PM	55 minutes
11:00 AM	3:08 PM	4 hours, 8 minutes
5:45 AM	8:05 AM	2 hours, 20 minutes
8:42 PM	9:50 PM	1 hour, 8 minutes
5:14 AM	11:09 AM	5 hours, 55 minutes
5:12 PM	7:19 PM	2 hours, 7 minutes
7:28 AM	9:15 AM	1 hour, 47 minutes
5:19 AM	9:17 PM	15 hours, 58 minutes
5:33 AM	8:15 PM	14 hours, 42 minutes

B. Solve the word problem.

Kayla's father said she had to clean her room before she could go to her friend's house. Kayla started cleaning at 10:15 AM. It took her 17 minutes to pick up her clothes and put them away neatly. She spent 24 minutes organizing her bookshelf. It took her 9 minutes to clean under her bed and 8 minutes to change her sheets. Then she spent 22 minutes vacuuming and dusting. Finally, Kayla was done and went to her friend's house.

1. How long did Kayla spend cleaning her room? 1 hour, 20 minutes
2. At what time did she go to her friend's house? 11:35 AM

Friday WEEK 3 43

Page 44

Geography

Africa's Bodies of Water

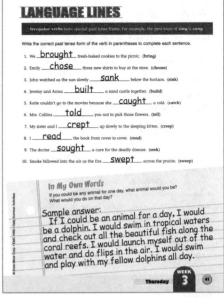

Use the map to answer the questions.

1. Which lake is the largest in Africa? Lake Victoria
2. Which river is the longest in Africa? Nile River
3. Which sea is east of the Nile River? Red Sea
4. Which river is farthest south? Zambezi River
5. Which body of water separates mainland Africa from its largest island? Mozambique Channel
6. Which two oceans border Africa? Atlantic Ocean and Indian Ocean

44 Friday

Week 4

Page 47

Read It! Fiction

Read the story. Then answer the questions.

Prometheus

In ancient Greek mythology, Prometheus was a Titan, one of the most powerful gods. Yet even though he was a god, he found humans interesting. Zeus, the ruler of all the gods, did not care about human struggles, but Prometheus wanted to help the mortals.

According to the myths, Prometheus looked for ways to help humans solve their problems. For example, he taught people how to make bricks to build homes, how to tell the seasons by looking at the stars, and how to navigate ships. Humans, with the help of Prometheus's knowledge, began to advance. They became more independent.

Zeus ordered Prometheus to stop helping the humans, but Prometheus continued. After Prometheus stole fire from Zeus and gave it to the people, Zeus grew incredibly angry. Until then, he alone had controlled fire. By giving it to the humans, Prometheus was offering them the final power they needed to grow and prosper without the help of the gods.

Zeus was furious. "You dared to defy me?" he cried. "You brought fire to those too foolish to use it properly. Now you must be punished!" Zeus chained Prometheus to a mountain and sent an eagle to tear at his flesh. While Prometheus remained bound and helpless, the eagle ate his liver. Each day, the liver grew back, and the eagle attacked it anew.

Prometheus's torture continued for years. Finally, brave Heracles, Zeus's son, could no longer stand to see Prometheus suffer. Heracles killed the eagle and set Prometheus free.

1. **Which of these statements best tells the main idea of the passage?**
   - Ⓐ Zeus and Prometheus fought about Heracles.
   - Ⓑ Zeus told Prometheus to avoid humans.
   - Ⓒ Prometheus was chained to a mountain, and an eagle ate his liver.
   - ● Prometheus disobeyed Zeus by sharing knowledge with humans.
2. **Which of these is the main idea of the second paragraph?**
   - ● Prometheus wanted to see humans prosper.
   - Ⓑ Prometheus thought humans were foolish.
   - Ⓒ Zeus kept Prometheus away from humans.
   - Ⓓ Prometheus helped humans, but they were ungrateful.
3. **Which detail explains why Zeus finally decided to punish Prometheus?**
   - ● Prometheus gave fire to humans.
   - Ⓑ Prometheus was a Titan.
   - Ⓒ Prometheus taught humans to make bricks and build homes.
   - Ⓓ Prometheus got help from Heracles.
4. **Which of these details shows that Prometheus's torture was ongoing?**
   - Ⓐ Zeus chained Prometheus to a mountain.
   - ● Prometheus's liver grew back, and the eagle attacked it repeatedly.
   - Ⓒ Prometheus was bound and helpless.
   - Ⓓ Heracles killed the eagle and freed Prometheus.

Monday WEEK 4 47

Page 48

Write It Right

Rewrite each sentence, correcting the errors.

1. after we goes to the mall, than lets get sum Pizza
   After we go to the mall, then let's get some pizza.
2. Look at all them children playing, in the fountin!
   Look at all those children playing in the fountain!
3. taylor and emily checks out sevin books at the libary yesterday
   Taylor and Emily checked out seven books at the library yesterday.
4. joshua asks me to goes to the dance last wensday
   Joshua asked me to go to the dance last Wednesday.

MATH TIME

Use the clues to find each number.

1. • This number is a mixed number. • When this number is multiplied by $\frac{3}{4}$, the product is $1\frac{1}{8}$. $1\frac{1}{2}$	2. • This number is a mixed number. • When this number is divided by $\frac{2}{5}$, the answer is $8\frac{1}{2}$. $3\frac{2}{5}$	3. • This number is a mixed number. • When this number is multiplied by $\frac{1}{3}$, the product is $1\frac{2}{5}$. $4\frac{1}{5}$

48 Monday

Page 49

SPELL IT

Many words have consonants that are **silent**. For example, the t is silent in the word **hustle**.

Fill in the letters to complete the spelling words for the week. Then circle the silent consonant in each word.

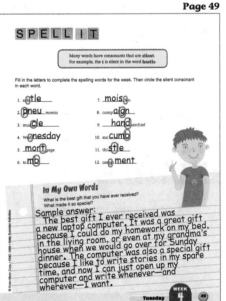

1. subtle
2. pneumonia
3. muscle
4. Wednesday
5. mortgage
6. tomb
7. moisten
8. campaign
9. handkerchief
10. succumb
11. thistle
12. assignment

In My Own Words

What is the best gift that you have ever received? What made it so special?

Sample answer:
The best gift I ever received was a new laptop computer. It was a great gift because I could do my homework on my bed, in the living room, or even at my grandma's house when we would go over for Sunday dinner. The computer was also a special gift because I like to write stories in my spare time, and now I can just open up my computer and write whenever—and wherever—I want.

Tuesday WEEK 4 49

© Evan-Moor Corp. • EMC 1068 • Daily Summer Activities

LANGUAGE LINES

A group of words that expresses a complete thought is called a **sentence**. A group of words that does not express a complete thought is called a **fragment**.

Write *sentence* or *fragment* after each group of words.

1. Andrew went to the store with his mother. — sentence
2. Ate lunch together in the cafeteria. — fragment
3. My little brother and his friends from school. — fragment
4. The mosquitoes, they were everywhere. — sentence
5. We always go to the movies on Saturday. — sentence
6. When all of the people in my neighborhood gather. — fragment
7. Knows how to put together a kite. — fragment
8. She ate. — sentence

MATH TIME

Measure the length of each writing tool to the nearest quarter inch.

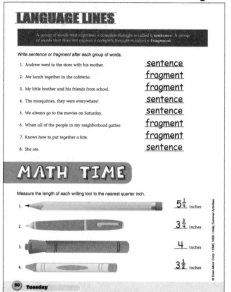

1. $5\frac{1}{4}$ inches
2. $3\frac{3}{4}$ inches
3. 4 inches
4. $3\frac{1}{2}$ inches

Read It! Nonfiction

Read the article and study the diagram. Then answer the questions.

Parts of the Eye

The human eye is a remarkable system of sensitive parts. These tiny tissues work together to send messages to the brain.

First, light rays enter the eye through the transparent **cornea**. The rays then pass through the **pupil**, which changes size to adjust to different light levels. The pupil dilates, or becomes bigger, in dark rooms and will contract, or become smaller, in brightly lit places.

The **iris** is the colored part of the eye, and it controls the opening and closing of the pupil. Irises can be blue, green, brown, gray, or hazel.

The **lens** focuses the light rays on the **retina**. The retina is tissue at the back of the eye that is sensitive to light. Nerves in the retina convert light energy into electrical energy, which is sent along the **optic nerve** to the brain. The brain interprets the electrical energy as an image.

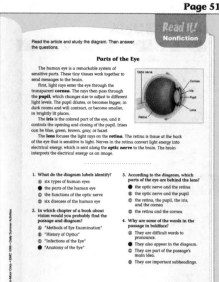

1. What do the diagram labels identify?
   Ⓐ six types of human eyes
   ● the parts of the human eye
   Ⓒ the functions of the optic nerve
   Ⓓ six diseases of the human eye

2. In which chapter of a book about vision would you probably find the passage and diagram?
   Ⓐ "Methods of Eye Examination"
   Ⓑ "History of Optics"
   Ⓒ "Infections of the Eye"
   ● "Anatomy of the Eye"

3. According to the diagram, which parts of the eye are behind the lens?
   Ⓐ the optic nerve and the retina
   Ⓑ the optic nerve and the pupil
   ● the retina, the pupil, the iris, and the cornea
   Ⓓ the retina and the cornea

4. Why are some of the words in the passage in boldface?
   Ⓐ They are difficult words to pronounce.
   Ⓑ They also appear in the diagram.
   ● They are part of the passage's main idea.
   Ⓓ They are important subheadings.

Vo·cab·u·lar·y

Heteronyms are words that are spelled the same but have different meanings and pronunciations. They can also be different parts of speech.

contract: con-TRAKT: (v.), "to shrink"   **contract:** CON-trakt: (n.), "an agreement"

Choose the correct heteronym for each pair of definitions. Then write the correct pronunciation next to each definition. Capital letters indicate emphasis.

digest: dī-JEST, DĪ-jest   **permit:** pur-MIT, PUR-mit
invalid: in-VAL-id, IN-vuh-lid   **perfect:** pur-FEKT, PUR-fikt
subject: sub-JEKT, SUB-jekt   **console:** kun-SOHL, KON-sohl
entrance: en-TRANSS, EN-trinss   **incense:** in-SENSS, IN-senss
minute: mī-NOOT, MIN-it   **refuse:** ree-FYOOZ, REF-yooss

1. a substance that smells nice when burned (n.) — IN-senss
   to make angry (v.) — in-SENSS
2. to spellbind (v.) — en-TRANSS
   where one enters (n.) — EN-trinss
3. a sickly person (n.) — IN-vuh-lid
   not true or correct (adj.) — in-VAL-id
4. sixty seconds (n.) — MIN-it
   tiny (adj.) — mī-NOOT
5. to say no (v.) — ree-FYOOZ
   garbage (n.) — REF-yooss
6. flawless (adj.) — PUR-fikt
   to make flawless (v.) — pur-FEKT
7. a collection of short articles or stories (n.) — DĪ-jest
   to process food (v.) — dī-JEST
8. to allow (v.) — pur-MIT
   a license (n.) — PUR-mit
9. to give comfort (v.) — kun-SOHL
   the control unit of an electronic system (n.) — KON-sohl
10. a topic or theme (n.) — SUB-jekt
    to expose to something (v.) — sub-JEKT

LANGUAGE LINES

A pronoun is used to replace a noun.

Read the paragraphs. Write the correct pronouns above the underlined words. The first one has been done for you.

They
Nicole and Aaron are at the library. Nicole and Aaron both have reports to finish. Nicole is **her**
writing about ancient Egypt. To start Nicole's research, Nicole read books about **She** **it** **she**
ancient Egypt. Nicole also watched a video about ancient Egypt. Aaron told Nicole that Nicole must **him** **she**
be turning into an expert. She told Aaron that Aaron would like to visit Egypt.

She
Aaron is writing about cats for science. Mrs. Armstrong, the librarian, brought Aaron and Nicole **they**
the books that Aaron and Nicole requested. Mrs. Armstrong explained that cats were important to the **he**
Egyptians. Aaron decided that Aaron would like to go to Egypt, too. Nicole told Aaron that Aaron and **we**
Nicole should go together. When I saw Aaron and Nicole, Nicole suggested that Nicole, Aaron, and I **them**
all go to Egypt. I said Egypt is too far away to travel to this afternoon!

In My Own Words

Describe your favorite place. Why do you like it so much? Use as much detail as you can.

Sample answer:
My favorite place is a field across the street from my house. As a young child, I used to go exploring in the field, hiding in the tall grass or climbing the apple trees that line the back of the land. During the spring, my friends and I would hunt for frogs in the small pond in the middle of the field. And during wintertime, we would ice skate on that pond and slide down the steep hills in our sleds.

Mind Jigglers

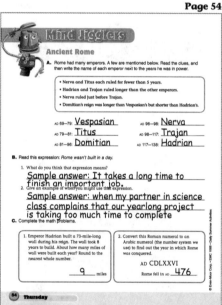

Ancient Rome

A. Rome had many emperors. A few are mentioned below. Read the clues, and then write the name of each emperor next to the years he was in power.

- Nerva and Titus each ruled for fewer than 5 years.
- Hadrian and Trajan ruled longer than the other emperors.
- Nerva ruled just before Trajan.
- Domitian's reign was longer than Vespasian's but shorter than Hadrian's.

AD 69–79: **Vespasian**   AD 96–98: **Nerva**
AD 79–81: **Titus**   AD 98–117: **Trajan**
AD 81–96: **Domitian**   AD 117–138: **Hadrian**

B. Read this expression: *Rome wasn't built in a day.*

1. What do you think that expression means?
   Sample answer: It takes a long time to finish an important job.

2. Give an example of when you might use that expression.
   Sample answer: when my partner in science class complains that our yearlong project is taking too much time to complete

C. Complete the math problems.

1. Emperor Hadrian built a 73-mile-long wall during his reign. The wall took 8 years to build. About how many miles of wall were built each year? Round to the nearest whole number.
   9 miles

2. Convert this Roman numeral to an Arabic numeral (the number system we use) to find out the year in which Rome was conquered.
   AD CDLXXVI
   Rome fell in AD **476**

MATH TIME

Circle Graph

There are 200 customers at the Soda Shop last Saturday. Mrs. McCool kept track of the number of people who bought each type of soda she sold. Here are the results:

Chocolate: 70 customers	**Root Beer:** 50 customers
Strawberry: 34 customers	**Vanilla:** 16 customers
Orange: 10 customers	**Cherry:** 20 customers

Use the information above to complete the circle graph and the key. Color each section of the graph a different color. Be sure the colors on your graph match the data and your key.

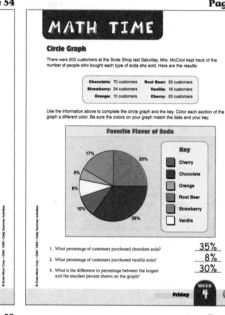

Favorite Flavor of Soda

Key:
- Cherry
- Chocolate
- Orange
- Root Beer
- Strawberry
- Vanilla

1. What percentage of customers purchased chocolate soda? — **35%**
2. What percentage of customers purchased vanilla soda? — **8%**
3. What is the difference in percentage between the largest and the smallest percent shown on the graph? — **30%**

Geography

Most Populated Countries in Europe

Use the color key to color in each country. Then write a caption for the map, stating a fact about Europe's population.

Country	Population	Country	Population
European Russia	108,724,360	Ukraine	45,415,596
Germany	82,282,988	Spain	40,548,753
France	64,768,389	Poland	38,463,689
United Kingdom	61,284,806	Romania	22,181,287
Italy	58,090,681	Netherlands	16,783,092

Color Key
Largest population: red
Smallest population: orange
Populations 50 to 79 million: green
Populations 40 to 49 million: blue
Populations 20 to 39 million: purple
Country ranked second in population: yellow

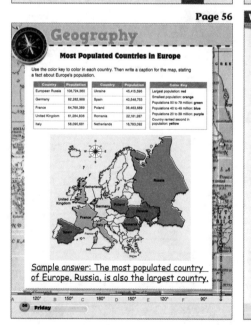

Sample answer: The most populated country of Europe, Russia, is also the largest country.

Read It! Fiction

Read the journal entries. Then answer the questions.

The Whale Watch

Jeongsoo and Samuel went on a whale-watching trip to Cape Cod, Massachusetts, with their class. They each wrote an account of what they saw and did.

Jeongsoo's Account
I had looked forward to our Cape Cod whale-watching trip all year. When we finally got on the boat, I thought, "This is it!" After a year of studying everything about whales, we were finally going to see them. Being on the boat was great. It was sunny and windy, the waves were enormous, and it wasn't long before we noticed our first whale, a huge finback that spouted water up through its blowhole just a few feet from the boat. We saw 12 whales altogether, including minke whales, humpbacks, and the endangered right whale. And I got videos of them all on my cell phone! They were the most amazing creatures I'd ever seen.

Samuel's Account
All year our class had studied whales, and I worked really hard learning about them and about the ocean. I could hardly wait to see the whales in their own habitat, so I was excited when we finally got to the boat. The waves were huge, though, and when the boat started moving, I began to feel weird. Then I got nauseated—really, really nauseated. I spent the whole day miserable with seasickness, curled up in a chair inside the cabin. I heard everyone shouting as the whales breached and spouted, but I missed it all. Luckily, Jeongsoo filmed the whales with his cell phone, so I got to see his video. The whales really were awesome.

1. What is one similarity between Jeongsoo's and Samuel's experiences?
   Ⓐ They both got really sick.
   Ⓑ They both had a great time.
   ● They both looked forward to the trip.
   Ⓓ They both sat in the ship's cabin.

2. Samuel's time on the boat was different from Jeongsoo's because Samuel
   Ⓐ saw a whale spout
   ● did not see any whales during the trip
   Ⓒ had studied whales all year
   Ⓓ had a cell phone

3. The boys both thought that the ___
   ● whales were amazing
   Ⓑ trip was fun
   Ⓒ boat movement was sickening
   Ⓓ humpback whale was huge

4. Jeongsoo's experience was more enjoyable than Samuel's because Jeongsoo
   ● learned more about whales in school
   Ⓑ went to Cape Cod
   Ⓒ did not get sick
   Ⓓ had a better seat on the ship

Write It Right

Rewrite each sentence, correcting the errors.

1. No body couldn't tell us, wear the blew house was
   Nobody could tell us where the blue house was.

2. may I please have some more potatos spinach and corn the little boy asked
   "May I please have some more potatoes, spinach, and corn?" the little boy asked.

3. Mr and mrs tyler left for hawaii on friday august 25th and returned the following week
   Mr. and Mrs. Tyler left for Hawaii on Friday, August 25th, and returned the following week.

MATH TIME

Round each of these numbers to the specified place value.

1. 280 to the nearest hundred — **300**
2. 49,305 to the nearest thousand — **49,000**
3. 27,539 to the nearest ten — **27,540**
4. 184,390 to the nearest ten thousand — **180,000**
5. 286,952 to the nearest hundred thousand — **300,000**
6. 1,682,842 to the nearest hundred thousand — **1,700,000**
7. 5,930,206 to the nearest million — **6,000,000**

Page 61

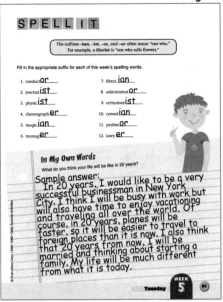

SPELL IT

The suffixes **-ian**, **-ist**, **-er**, and **-or** often mean "one who." For example, a **florist** is "one who sells flowers."

Fill in the appropriate suffix for each of this week's spelling words.

1. conduct**or**
2. journal**ist**
3. physic**ist**
4. choreograph**er**
5. magic**ian**
6. manag**er**
7. librar**ian**
8. administrat**or**
9. orthodont**ist**
10. comed**ian**
11. profess**or**
12. lawy**er**

In My Own Words

What do you think your life will be like in 20 years?

Sample answer: In 20 years, I would like to be a very successful businessman in New York City. I think I will be busy with work but will also have time to enjoy vacationing and traveling all over the world. Of course, in 20 years, planes will be faster, so it will be easier to travel to foreign places than it is now. I also think that 20 years from now, I will be married and thinking about starting a family. My life will be much different from what it is today.

© Evan-Moor Corp. • EMC 1068 • Daily Summer Activities

Tuesday WEEK 5 61

Page 62

LANGUAGE LINES

Words that measure weight, length, and volume are often written as **abbreviations**.

Write the letter of the correct abbreviation next to its measurement word.

c	1. pound	a. mL
g	2. kilometer	b. qt.
a	3. milliliter	c. lb.
j	4. mile	d. kg
h	5. centigram	e. L
b	6. quart	f. cm
i	7. ounce	g. km
d	8. kilogram	h. cg
e	9. liter	i. oz.
f	10. centimeter	j. mi.

MATH TIME

Solve each equation. Show all of your work. The first one has been done for you.

1. $x + 4 = 53$ — $x = 53 - 4$, $x = 49$ — $x =$ **49**
2. $x + 27 = 368$ — $x =$ **341**
3. $x + 18 = 12$ — $x =$ **-6**
4. $(x + 5) + 5 = 11$ — $x =$ **1**
5. $x - 6 = 21$ — $x =$ **27**
6. $x - 15 = -4$ — $x =$ **11**
7. $x - 44 = 13$ — $x =$ **57**
8. $(x - 9) + 17 = 12$ — $x =$ **4**

62 Tuesday

© Evan-Moor Corp. • EMC 1068 • Daily Summer Activities

Page 63

Read It! Nonfiction

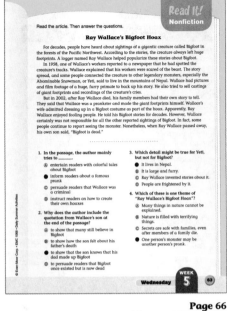

Read the article. Then answer the questions.

Ray Wallace's Bigfoot Hoax

For decades, people have heard about sightings of a gigantic creature called Bigfoot in the forests of the Pacific Northwest. According to the stories, the creature always left huge footprints. A logger named Ray Wallace helped popularize these stories about Bigfoot.

In 1958, one of Wallace's workers reported to a newspaper that he had spotted the creature's tracks. Wallace explained that his workers were scared of the beast. The story spread, and some people connected the creature to other legendary monsters, especially the Abominable Snowman, or Yeti, said to live in the mountains of Nepal. Wallace had pictures and film footage of a huge, furry primate to back up his story. He also tried to sell castings of giant footprints and recordings of the creature's cries.

But in 2002, after Ray Wallace died, his family members had their own story to tell. They said that Wallace was a prankster and made the giant footprints himself. Wallace's wife admitted dressing up in a Bigfoot costume as part of the hoax. Apparently, Ray Wallace enjoyed fooling people. He told his Bigfoot stories for decades. However, Wallace certainly was not responsible for all the other reported sightings of Bigfoot. In fact, some people continue to report seeing the monster. Nonetheless, when Ray Wallace passed away, his own son said, "Bigfoot is dead."

1. **In the passage, the author mainly tries to ______.**
   - Ⓐ entertain readers with colorful tales about Bigfoot
   - ● inform readers about a famous prank
   - Ⓒ persuade readers that Wallace was a criminal
   - Ⓓ instruct readers on how to create their own hoaxes
2. **Why does the author include the quotation from Wallace's son at the end of the passage?**
   - Ⓐ to show that many still believe in Bigfoot
   - Ⓑ to show how the son felt about his father's death
   - ● to show that the son knows that his dad made up Bigfoot
   - Ⓓ to persuade readers that Bigfoot once existed but is now dead
3. **Which detail might be true for Yeti, but not for Bigfoot?**
   - ● It lives in Nepal.
   - Ⓑ It is large and furry.
   - Ⓒ Ray Wallace invented stories about it.
   - Ⓓ People are frightened by it.
4. **Which of these is one theme of "Ray Wallace's Bigfoot Hoax"?**
   - Ⓐ Many things in nature cannot be explained.
   - Ⓑ Nature is filled with terrifying things.
   - Ⓒ Secrets are safe with families, even after members of a family die.
   - ● One person's monster may be another person's prank.

© Evan-Moor Corp. • EMC 1068 • Daily Summer Activities

Wednesday WEEK 5 63

Page 64

Vo•cab•u•lar•y

Synonyms are words that have almost the same meaning. You can use synonyms to vary your writing or to make your language more precise.

Pursue is a synonym for **chase**.
Confirm is a synonym for **prove**.

A. Write the letter of the correct synonym next to each word. Use a dictionary to help you.

f	1. happy	a. encroach
d	2. approve	b. entice
h	3. burden	c. intimidate
a	4. trespass	d. endorse
c	5. threaten	e. valiant
b	6. tempt	f. elated
e	7. courageous	g. tenacity
g	8. determination	h. encumber

B. For each word, find the synonym given for it above. Then write a sentence using the synonym.

1. burden: Sample answer: Rylee was encumbered by a backpack stuffed with many books.
2. tempt: Sample answer: Marcia tried to entice me with one of her delicious homemade cupcakes.
3. happy: Sample answer: Julia's parents were elated about the news of her engagement.
4. determination: Sample answer: Dustin showed real tenacity when he battled back from a slow start and won the race.

© Evan-Moor Corp. • EMC 1068 • Daily Summer Activities

64 Wednesday

Page 65

LANGUAGE LINES

Use a comma before or after a person's name if he or she is being addressed directly.

Ryan, what time is it? It is three o'clock, Emma.

Rewrite these sentences correctly, adding commas where they are needed.

1. Kaya have you finished your chores?
   Kaya, have you finished your chores?
2. I think I have Ben.
   I think I have, Ben.
3. Kaya let's get Dad to drive us to the mall.
   Kaya, let's get Dad to drive us to the mall.
4. Dad can you take Ben and me to the mall?
   Dad, can you take Ben and me to the mall?

In My Own Words

Name a book you have read that you think should be made into a movie. Why would this book make a good movie?

Sample answer: I think the book A Wrinkle in Time by Madeleine L'Engle would make a great movie. It's a story about a teenage girl, Meg, whose father has mysteriously gone missing on a scientific government mission. Meg, her intellectually gifted younger brother Charles Wallace, and new friend Calvin are visited by three strange old women who take them on a trip through space and time to save Meg's father.

© Evan-Moor Corp. • EMC 1068 • Daily Summer Activities

Thursday WEEK 5 65

Page 66

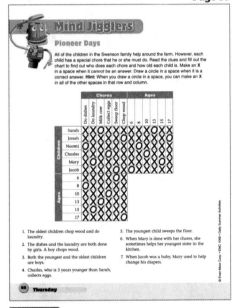

Mind Jigglers

Pioneer Days

All of the children in the Swenson family help around the farm. However, each child has a special chore that he or she must do. Read the clues and fill out the chart to find out who does each chore and how old each child is. Make an **X** in a space when it *cannot* be an answer. Draw a circle in a space when it is a correct answer. **Hint:** When you draw a circle in a space, you can make an **X** in all of the other spaces in that row and column.

		Chores						Ages					
		Do dishes	Do laundry	Milk cow	Collect eggs	Sweep floor	Chop wood	6	8	10	13	15	17
Children	Sarah	X	X	O	X	X	X	X	X	X	O	X	X
	Jonah	X	X	X	X	X	O	X	X	X	X	X	O
	Naomi	O	X	X	X	X	X	X	O	X	X	X	X
	Charles	X	X	X	O	X	X	X	X	O	X	X	X
	Mary	X	O	X	X	X	X	X	X	X	X	O	X
	Jacob	X	X	X	X	O	X	O	X	X	X	X	X
Ages	6	X	X	X	X	O	X						
	8	O	X	X	X	X	X						
	10	X	X	X	O	X	X						
	13	X	X	O	X	X	X						
	15	X	O	X	X	X	X						
	17	X	X	X	X	X	O						

1. The oldest children chop wood and do laundry.
2. The dishes and the laundry are both done by girls. A boy chops wood.
3. Both the youngest and the oldest children are boys.
4. Charles, who is 3 years younger than Sarah, collects eggs.
5. The youngest child sweeps the floor.
6. When Mary is done with her chores, she sometimes helps her youngest sister in the kitchen.
7. When Jacob was a baby, Mary used to help change his diapers.

© Evan-Moor Corp. • EMC 1068 • Daily Summer Activities

66 Thursday

Page 67

MATH TIME

Reducing Fractions

One way to reduce fractions to their lowest terms is to find the Greatest Common Factor (GCF) of the numerator and the denominator. Divide both fractions by the GCF and you have reduced them to lowest terms.

The GCF of 12 and 20 is 4. Divide both the numerator and denominator by 4.

$$\frac{12}{20} = \frac{12 \div 4}{20 \div 4} = \frac{3}{5}$$

Find the GCF of each numerator and denominator. Then reduce the fraction. The first one has been done for you.

	GCF	Reduced Fraction
1. $\frac{3}{9} \div$	$\frac{3}{3}$	$\frac{1}{3}$
2. $\frac{8}{12} \div$	$\frac{4}{4}$	$\frac{2}{3}$
3. $\frac{10}{25} \div$	$\frac{5}{5}$	$\frac{2}{5}$
4. $\frac{15}{20} \div$	$\frac{5}{5}$	$\frac{3}{4}$
5. $\frac{4}{50} \div$	$\frac{2}{2}$	$\frac{2}{25}$
6. $\frac{13}{39} \div$	$\frac{13}{13}$	$\frac{1}{3}$
7. $\frac{12}{15} \div$	$\frac{3}{3}$	$\frac{4}{5}$
8. $\frac{20}{24} \div$	$\frac{4}{4}$	$\frac{5}{6}$
9. $\frac{15}{60} \div$	$\frac{15}{15}$	$\frac{1}{4}$
10. $\frac{36}{42} \div$	$\frac{6}{6}$	$\frac{6}{7}$

© Evan-Moor Corp. • EMC 1068 • Daily Summer Activities

Friday WEEK 5 67

Page 68

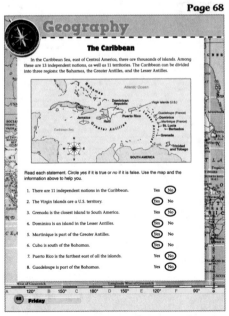

Geography

The Caribbean

In the Caribbean Sea, east of Central America, there are thousands of islands. Among these are 13 independent nations, as well as 11 territories. The Caribbean can be divided into three regions: the Bahamas, the Greater Antilles, and the Lesser Antilles.

Read each statement. Circle *yes* if it is true or *no* if it is false. Use the map and the information above to help you.

1. There are 11 independent nations in the Caribbean. Yes **(No)**
2. The Virgin Islands are a U.S. territory. **(Yes)** No
3. Grenada is the closest island to South America. Yes **(No)**
4. Dominica is an island in the Lesser Antilles. **(Yes)** No
5. Martinique is part of the Greater Antilles. **(Yes)** No
6. Cuba is south of the Bahamas. **(Yes)** No
7. Puerto Rico is the farthest east of all the islands. Yes **(No)**
8. Guadeloupe is part of the Bahamas. Yes **(No)**

68 Friday

Week 6 — Page 71

Read It! Fiction

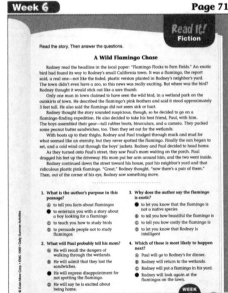

Read the story. Then answer the questions.

A Wild Flamingo Chase

Rodney read the headline in the local paper: "Flamingo Flocks to Fern Fields." An exotic bird had found its way to Rodney's small California town. It was a flamingo, the report said, a real one—not like the faded, plastic version planted in Rodney's neighbor's yard. The town didn't even have a zoo, so this news was really exciting. But where was the bird? Rodney thought it would stick out like a sore thumb.

Only one man in town claimed to have seen the wild bird, in a wetland park on the outskirts of town. He described the flamingo's pink feathers and said it stood approximately 3 feet tall. He also said the flamingo did not seem sick or hurt.

Rodney thought the story sounded suspicious, though, so he decided to go on a flamingo-finding expedition. He also decided to take his best friend, Paul, with him. The boys assembled their gear—tall rubber boots, binoculars, and a camera. They packed some peanut butter sandwiches, too. Then they set out for the wetlands.

With boots up to their thighs, Rodney and Paul trudged through muck and mud for what seemed like an eternity, but they never spotted the flamingo. Finally the sun began to set, and a cold wind cut through the boys' jackets. Rodney and Paul decided to head home.

As they turned onto Paul's street, they saw Paul's mom waiting on the porch. Paul dragged his feet up the driveway. His mom put her arm around him, and the two went inside.

Rodney continued down the street toward his house, past his neighbor's yard and that ridiculous plastic pink flamingo. "Great," Rodney thought, "now there's a pair of them." Then, out of the corner of his eye, Rodney saw something move.

1. **What is the author's purpose in this passage?**
   - Ⓐ to tell you facts about flamingos
   - ● to entertain you with a story about a boy looking for a flamingo
   - Ⓒ to teach you how to study birds
   - Ⓓ to persuade people not to study flamingos
2. **What will Paul probably tell his mom?**
   - Ⓐ He will recall the dangers of walking through the wetlands.
   - Ⓑ He will admit that they lost the sandwiches.
   - ● He will express disappointment for not spotting the flamingo.
   - Ⓓ He will say he is excited about being home.
3. **Why does the author say the flamingo is *exotic*?**
   - ● to let you know that the flamingo is not a native species
   - Ⓑ to tell you how beautiful the flamingo is
   - Ⓒ to tell you how costly the flamingo is
   - Ⓓ to let you know that Rodney is intelligent
4. **Which of these is most likely to happen next?**
   - Ⓐ Paul will go to Rodney's for dinner.
   - Ⓑ Rodney will return to the wetlands.
   - Ⓒ Rodney will put a flamingo in his yard.
   - ● Rodney will look again at the flamingos on the lawn.

© Evan-Moor Corp. • EMC 1068 • Daily Summer Activities

Monday WEEK 6 71

Write It Right

Rewrite each sentence, correcting the errors.

1. Lets all go too the carnival, "said james"
   "Let's all go to the carnival," said James.

2. Brad and angie wood not share, they're chips with jennifer
   Brad and Angie would not share their chips with Jennifer.

3. I atend mark twain jr hi in redmond washington
   I attend Mark Twain Junior High in Redmond, Washington.

4. We goes to Jame's house after scool tommorrow
   We will go to James's house after school tomorrow.

MATH TIME

Plot each of the following points on the number line and label them with the corresponding letters. The letters will spell out a favorite swimming activity.

$4\frac{1}{8}$ A		2.6 C	
7.8 O		$9\frac{1}{2}$ B	
$5\frac{7}{10}$ N		$11\frac{4}{5}$ A	
$14\frac{2}{8}$ L		13.2 L	
8.5 N		6.4 N	

C A N N O N B A L L
0 1 2 3 4 5 6 7 8 9 10 11 12 13 14 15 16

SPELL IT

The /sh/ sound is sometimes spelled xi, ci, ti, or si.

Fill in the correct letters that stand for the /sh/ sound in the spelling words for the week.

1. an**xi**__ous
2. distinc**ti**__on
3. suffi**ci**__ent
4. essen**ti**__al
5. obno**xi**__ous
6. espe**ci**__ally
7. transi**ti**__onal
8. intermis**si**__on
9. discus**si**__on
10. benefi**ci**__al
11. poten**ti**__al
12. depres**si**__on

In My Own Words

Write about something you would like to invent that would make life easier for people.

Sample answer:
I would like to invent the ability to teleport. That way, we would not have to drive or fly to get to school or go on vacation. We could walk to the nearest teleport station and then—poof!—arrive at our desired location in a matter of seconds. This would save people from being stuck in traffic, having to pay for gas, and having to spend time at an airport.

LANGUAGE LINES

An indefinite pronoun is a pronoun that refers to an unspecified person or thing.

Circle the indefinite pronoun that correctly completes each sentence.

1. We need _____ to help out this weekend for the class cleanup.   one   (everybody)   all
2. _____ have signed up for litter patrol in the park.   Each   (Several)   Other
3. Surprisingly, _____ has volunteered yet to work at the beach.   few   another   (no one)
4. _____ needs to pick up the trash there.   (Somebody)   Both   Most

MATH TIME

Find the area of each polygon. Reminder: The area of a triangle is ½ (base x height).

1. **8**
2. **20**
3. **24**
4. **16**
5. **10**
6. **6**
7. **30**
8. **16**

Read It! Nonfiction

Read the article. Then answer the questions.

The Brigantines

The sailing ships on which pirates traveled the seas long ago were magnificent boats. This diagram shows one common type of ship they used, called the *brigantine*, or *brig*. Many pirates in the 1700s preferred the brig because it was light and fast. It also had a large cargo hold for plenty of pirates' loot!

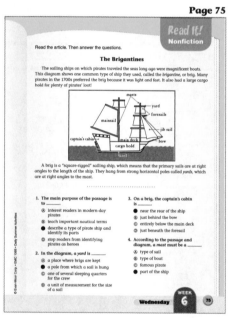

masts, yard, foresails, mainsail, jib sail, captain's cabin, main deck, bow, cargo hold, keel

A brig is a "square-rigged" sailing ship, which means that the primary sails are at right angles to the length of the ship. They hang from strong horizontal poles called *yards*, which are at right angles to the mast.

1. The main purpose of the passage is to _____
   Ⓐ interest readers in modern-day pirates
   Ⓑ teach important nautical terms
   ● describe a type of pirate ship and identify its parts
   Ⓓ stop readers from identifying pirates as heroes

2. In the diagram, a *yard* is _____
   Ⓐ a place where brigs are kept
   ● a pole from which a sail is hung
   Ⓒ one of several sleeping quarters for the crew
   Ⓓ a unit of measurement for the size of a sail

3. On a brig, the captain's cabin is _____
   Ⓐ near the rear of the ship
   Ⓑ just behind the bow
   ● entirely below the main deck
   Ⓓ just beneath the foresail

4. According to the passage and diagram, a *mast* must be a _____
   Ⓐ type of sail
   ● type of boat
   Ⓒ famous pirate
   Ⓓ part of the ship

Vo·cab·u·lar·y

Using precise language makes your meaning clear and your writing more interesting. Choose carefully among synonyms to make your writing more precise.

Write the word for *think* that best fits each definition in parentheses and completes the sentence. Use a dictionary if necessary.

deduced	deems	suppose	theorizes	consider
imagining	assumes	pondering	hypothesized	contemplated

1. He **contemplated** what decision to make for a long time.
   (thought seriously about)

2. We were having a hard time **imagining** thousands of buffalo on the plains.
   (making a mental picture of)

3. I'm not sure it's the best idea, but I **suppose** we could jump.
   (believe)

4. Dr. Smith **theorizes** that the number of bugs was due to the heavy rain.
   (guesses or forms a theory)

5. Based on the evidence, I have **deduced** that the butler did it.
   (concluded)

6. I will **consider** all my options before choosing a summer camp.
   (think carefully about)

7. Copernicus **hypothesized** that Earth revolves around the sun.
   (proposed an idea to explain facts)

8. I was **pondering** the meaning of the question all night.
   (thinking deeply about)

9. Mom **assumes** I have homework every night.
   (takes for granted)

10. Lin **deems** that it's better to shower before bedtime than in the morning.
    (has an opinion)

LANGUAGE LINES

When the beginning sounds of several words in a phrase are the same, it is called alliteration.

Circle the words in each sentence that demonstrate alliteration.

1. Nobody knows how Nora's nicest shoes ended up in the puppy's bed.
2. The hazy hot humid weather made Henry Harvey feel like he was wrapped in a horribly heavy wet blanket.
3. Sheila shouldn't show everyone Sean's photographs without his permission.
4. We have many merry memories of Emily's musical madness parties.
5. Stella stared at the stars on Saturday evening.
6. Poor Paul paraded around town in an old pair of pajamas.

In My Own Words

What are the qualities of a good friend? Why are these things important?

Sample answer:
A good friend is loyal and kind and will always be there for you when you need him or her. A good friend makes you laugh and accepts you for who you are. Finally, a good friend tells you the truth, even if it's not what you want to hear.

Mind Jigglers

Supersize It!

A. List your answers to the following questions. Sample answers:

1. Besides the planet itself, what do you think are three of the biggest things in the world?	2. What are three things that you wish were bigger than they are?
oceans	my room
mountains	the park in town
deserts	my TV

B. Make up a question that could have the given answer. Write the question on the line.

1. The answer is **not very big**. What might the question be? Sample answers:
   How big are newborn kittens?

2. The answer is **about as big as me**. What might the question be?
   How big is your twin sister?

C. Use the clues to name these big things.

"blank" of China: G**reat** w**all**
biggest mammal: b**lue** w**hale**
large house: m**ansion**
big meal: f**east**
longest river: N**ile**
largest U.S. state: A**laska**
highest mountain: M**ount** E**verest**

D. Will is 3 inches shorter than Karen. Karen is 2 inches taller than Jack. Jack is 4 inches taller than Grace. Will is 62 inches tall. How tall, in inches, is each child?

Will: **62 inches**
Grace: **59 inches**
Jack: **63 inches**
Karen: **65 inches**

MATH TIME

You Draw the Lines

On each figure, draw its lines of symmetry. If there are no lines of symmetry, write the word *none* next to the figure. If there are lines of symmetry, write the number of lines next to the figure.

1. **2**
2. **4**
3. **none**
4. **2**
5. **4**
6. **1**
7. **4**
8. **none**

Geography

Gold and Diamonds in Africa

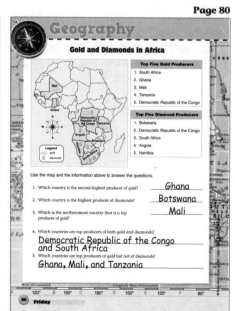

Top Five Gold Producers
1. South Africa
2. Ghana
3. Mali
4. Tanzania
5. Democratic Republic of the Congo

Top Five Diamond Producers
1. Botswana
2. Democratic Republic of the Congo
3. South Africa
4. Angola
5. Namibia

Use the map and the information above to answer the questions.

1. Which country is the second-highest producer of gold? **Ghana**
2. Which country is the highest producer of diamonds? **Botswana**
3. Which is the northernmost country that is a top producer of gold? **Mali**
4. Which countries are top producers of both gold and diamonds?
   Democratic Republic of the Congo and South Africa
5. Which countries are top producers of gold but not of diamonds?
   Ghana, Mali, and Tanzania

Answer Key 135

Page 83

Read It! Fiction

Read the story. Then answer the questions.

The Greedy Tiger and the Big Wind

Long ago, the rains did not fall, and there was a terrible drought. It was hard to find food, and the animals became hungry and thirsty. Only one tree had fruit. It was a big, beautiful pear tree that grew in the middle of a field. Its roots reached deep into the earth, where they drank from an underground spring. Its pears were plump and juicy. The tree, however, was guarded by a cruel and greedy tiger. Although he couldn't possibly eat all the fruit that the tree provided, Tiger wouldn't let any of the other animals touch the pears.

The desperate animals went to Rabbit and asked for help. Rabbit helped them form a plan. Then he went to Tiger and said, "Tiger, a great wind is coming. It will be so strong that it will blow everyone off the earth!" While Rabbit talked to Tiger, the birds, which were hidden in the forest, began to flap their wings wildly, creating a strong breeze. Next, other animals beat on the ground and swung through the trees, causing the trees to sway and shake. Tiger believed that the great wind had come, and he was terrified.

"I will tie you down with rope so the wind cannot blow you away," Rabbit offered. Tiger agreed, and Rabbit tied him tightly to a tree. Finally, Rabbit called the other animals, who came out of the forest and ate every delicious pear on the tree, laughing at the selfish tiger who watched helplessly.

1. The animals of the forest grew very hungry after ______.
- Ⓐ Tiger ate all the juicy pears
- ● a drought came to the land
- Ⓒ the rains came to the land
- Ⓓ a great wind began to blow

2. Before Rabbit tied up Tiger, the animals ______.
- ● could not get to the pears
- Ⓑ ate all the pears
- Ⓒ laughed at Tiger
- Ⓓ came out of the forest

3. What did Rabbit have to do before the animals could eat?
- Ⓐ create a big wind
- Ⓑ make Tiger angry
- Ⓒ wait for the pears to ripen
- ● tie Tiger to a tree

4. What happened after the animals made noise in the forest?
- Ⓐ Tiger ran away in fear of the wind.
- ● Tiger allowed Rabbit to tie him up.
- Ⓒ Rabbit formed a plan.
- Ⓓ Rabbit warned Tiger about the wind.

Monday WEEK 7 83

Page 84

Write It Right

Rewrite each sentence, correcting the errors.

1. marco and his little brother gone to the beech and builded sand cassles
   Marco and his little brother went to the beach and built sand castles.
2. When the piñata breaked all the childs runned to get the candy?
   When the piñata broke, all the children ran to get the candy.
3. Lets wash the car and clean out the garage today. mother said
   "Let's wash the car and clean out the garage today," Mother said.
4. hanna and amy getted in to there moms jewelry draw
   Hanna and Amy got into their mom's jewelry drawer.

MATH TIME

Fill in the blanks to make each math sentence true.

1. 2 meters = 200 centimeters
2. 3 kilometers = 3,000 meters
3. 6 centimeters = 60 millimeters
4. 250 centimeters = 2.5 meters
5. 600 decimeters = 60 meters
6. 150 millimeters = 15 centimeters
7. 12 decimeters = 120 centimeters
8. $1\frac{3}{4}$ meters = 175 centimeters
9. 0.5 meters = 5 decimeters
10. 3 kilometers = 300,000 centimeters
11. 5.2 centimeters = 52 millimeters
12. 1.6 decimeters = 16 centimeters

84 Monday

Page 85

SPELL IT

Some English words are taken from other languages such as French, German, Spanish, and Hindu.

Circle the correct spelling for each of this week's spelling words.

1.	**(pajamas)**	pajammas	pijammas	7. chandileer	chandilier	**(chandelier)**
2.	boquet	**(bouquet)**	bouquat	8. gormet	**(gourmet)**	gormat
3.	delicattesen	**(delicatessen)**	delicutessin	9. **(burrito)**	buritto	burritto
4.	**(futon)**	fouton	futoun	10. guitaur	gitaur	**(guitar)**
5.	spagetti	spaggeti	**(spaghetti)**	11. bungallow	**(bungalow)**	bungalo
6.	**(sauerkraut)**	saurkraut	sourkraut	12. finaley	finalee	**(finale)**

In My Own Words

Describe the perfect meal. Use plenty of details to describe how it looks, smells, and tastes.

Sample answer:
The perfect meal is my mom's homemade pasta with meat sauce. Mom cooks up a big pot of ziti, which are slightly thick, cylindrical noodles. Over the noodles, she puts lots of chunky sauce with ground beef, pork, tomatoes, and herbs. The sauce is hearty and flavorful, with a hint of garlic. Then Mom sprinkles a little mozzarella cheese over the top. It melts and gets all gooey. That's my favorite part!

Tuesday WEEK 7 85

Page 86

LANGUAGE LINES

Parentheses can be used to enclose extra information within a sentence.

Add parentheses in these sentences where they are needed.

1. Jan's cousins Barb and Bev (who are also her best friends) held a party for her 75th birthday.
2. Make an appointment for your driver's test at the local DMV (Division of Motor Vehicles)
3. Please note that this bill must be paid in full within sixty (60) days.
4. Toni's favorite saying is "carpe diem" (KAR-pay DEE-um) which means "seize the day."
5. Louisa May Alcott (1832–1888) wrote the novels *Little Women* and *Jo's Boys.*
6. Find the Lowest Common Denominator (LCD) of the numbers.
7. The number of languages currently spoken on the planet (about 6,000) is decreasing.
8. The cartographers (mapmakers) of ancient times believed Earth was flat.

MATH TIME

A. Find the **range** of each set of data.

8, 5, 7, 8, 15, 23, 16	18
42, 61, 51, 54, 59, 57, 60, 53, 61	19
22, 24, 45, 31, 41, 38, 62, 26	40
5, 16, 11, 19, 41, 20, 39, 24, 27, 25	36

B. Find the **mean** of each set of data.

5, 8, 9, 11, 12, 15	10
25, 26, 29, 31, 33, 35, 38, 39	32
15, 18, 18, 19, 20, 23, 24, 25, 27	21
7, 8, 9, 13, 14, 15, 16, 18, 26	14

86 Tuesday

Page 87

Read It! Nonfiction

Read the article. Then answer the questions.

The Cliff Dwellers

Mesa Verde, which means "green table" in Spanish, is the name of a high plateau in Colorado. Made of sandstone and shale, this plateau rises almost 2,000 feet above the surrounding land. The mesa has many canyons with streams and rivers running through them. At the tops of the rocky canyon walls, there are many overhangs and cave-like alcoves that have formed from water seeping into the sandstone.

People first came to Mesa Verde sometime around AD 550. These early inhabitants dug into the floors of the alcoves, creating what are now called pit houses. Around AD 750, people moved out of the pit houses in the canyon walls and built above-ground houses from mud and stone. Then, around the year 1200, they returned to the alcoves in the canyon walls.

Nobody knows why the people returned to the cliff pit houses. They may have feared attack from other groups and believed the alcoves offered better protection. They may have wanted better shelter from the wind and blistering sun. Whatever the reason, the cliff dwellers stayed less than a hundred years in the pit houses after they had moved back.

By 1300, the cliff dwellings had been abandoned, probably because of a severe drought in the area. It wasn't until over four hundred years later that cowboys, trappers, and prospectors began to visit and photograph Mesa Verde, astonished by the sight of hundreds of cliff houses built into the walls of the canyons.

1. According to the passage, which event happened last?
- Ⓐ Mesa Verde inhabitants created pit houses.
- Ⓑ Water seeped into the rock and created alcoves.
- ● Cowboys, trappers, and prospectors learned of the cliff dwellings.
- Ⓓ Cliff dwellers abandoned the canyon walls because of drought.

2. What kind of homes did the Mesa Verde inhabitants first build?
- ● pit houses
- Ⓑ cave houses
- Ⓒ stone and mud houses
- Ⓓ wooden houses

3. The Mesa Verde inhabitants returned to the alcoves in canyon walls ______.
- Ⓐ before AD 550
- Ⓑ around AD 750
- ● around 1200
- Ⓓ after 1300

4. What were the last homes that the Mesa Verde people inhabited?
- Ⓐ cliff tops
- ● pit houses
- Ⓒ stone and mud houses
- Ⓓ wooden houses

Wednesday WEEK 7 87

Page 88

Vo·cab·u·lar·y

A **blended word** is created by combining parts of two or more words into one word. Blended words are also called "portmanteau words." A *portmanteau* is a suitcase that opens into two compartments.

A. Write the blended word that matches each clue.

picture + element = **pixel**	spoon + fork = **spork**
emotion + icon = **emoticon**	pulse + quasar = **pulsar**
guess + estimate = **guesstimate**	television + marathon = **telethon**
cybernetic + organism = **cyborg**	documentary + drama = **docudrama**
information + commercial = **infomercial**	simultaneous + broadcast = **simulcast**

1. a symbol that shows emotion in e-mails — emoticon
2. an artificial human — cyborg
3. a show on TV that explains a product — infomercial
4. a rotating star that emits pulsing waves — pulsar
5. a long fundraiser on TV — telethon
6. broadcast live on both TV and radio simultaneously — simulcast
7. an estimate based on a guess — guesstimate
8. one tiny unit of an image on a computer — pixel
9. a spoon-shaped eating utensil with fork-like prongs — spork
10. a TV or movie dramatization based on facts — docudrama

B. Write the blended word for each pair of words. Use a dictionary to help you, if necessary.

1. modulation + demodulation = modem
2. sports + broadcast = sportscast
3. fan + magazine = fanzine
4. smoke + fog = smog

88 Wednesday

Page 89

LANGUAGE LINES

Use commas to separate three or more items in a series.

Correct the sentences by adding commas where they are needed.

1. A human being's five senses are sight, hearing, touch, taste, and smell.
2. The cornea, the pupil, and the lens are three parts of the human eye.
3. The muscle known as the iris, the jelly-like substance called vitreous fluid, and the thumbnail-sized retina are other important eye parts.
4. The three main parts of the human ear are the canal, the eardrum, and the cochlea.
5. Hearing can be damaged by loud sounds, such as those made by jet planes, jackhammers, and highly amplified musical instruments.
6. A bacterial infection, a viral infection, or even an allergy can cause earaches.

In My Own Words

If you could control the weather, what would you do? Explain why.

Sample answer:
I would take a deep breath and blow away all the clouds and rain on days when I want sunshine, such as on my birthday and the last day of school. I would also shorten winter. Right after the holidays, I would turn up the heat so that spring could start in January!

Thursday WEEK 7 89

Page 90

Mind Jigglers

Invention Convention

A. Answer the questions to complete this sentence:
What has not yet been invented that would... Sample answers:

- change how we travel to places? flying cars
- make life easier at home? robots that can cook
- be good for the planet? a trash zapper that vaporizes garbage
- change how we communicate? a cell phone chip implanted directly into our brains
- be kind of silly? glasses that can turn into flashlights at night

B. What are three traits that an inventor should have? Sample answers:

1. creativity
2. intelligence
3. courage

C. Take a guess. In what year do you think each object was invented? Answers will vary.

- ballpoint pen ______
- vacuum cleaner ______
- zipper ______
- dishwasher ______
- safety pin ______
- stapler ______

Now do Activity D to see when they were actually invented.

D. Look at the dates listed below. Then use the clues to figure out what year each object was invented.

- The ballpoint pen was invented before the zipper.
- The safety pin and the vacuum cleaner were both invented in years that end in 9.
- The dishwasher was invented 2 years before the ballpoint pen.
- The stapler was invented 8 years after the vacuum cleaner.

1849: safety pin
1869: vacuum cleaner
1877: stapler
1886: dishwasher
1888: ballpoint pen
1891: zipper

90 Thursday

Page 91

MATH TIME

What's My Number?

Use the clues to find each number.

1. • My number is a mixed number.
   • When my number is multiplied by $\frac{3}{4}$, the product is $1\frac{1}{8}$. — $1\frac{1}{2}$
2. • My number is a mixed number.
   • When my number is divided by $\frac{2}{5}$, the answer is $8\frac{1}{2}$. — $3\frac{2}{5}$
3. • My number is a mixed number.
   • When my number is multiplied by $\frac{1}{3}$, the product is $1\frac{2}{5}$. — $4\frac{1}{5}$
4. • My number is *not* a mixed number.
   • When my number is divided by $\frac{1}{3}$, the answer is $1\frac{1}{2}$.
   • The numerator of my number is 1. — $\frac{1}{2}$

Friday WEEK 7 91

Page 92

Geography

East Asia

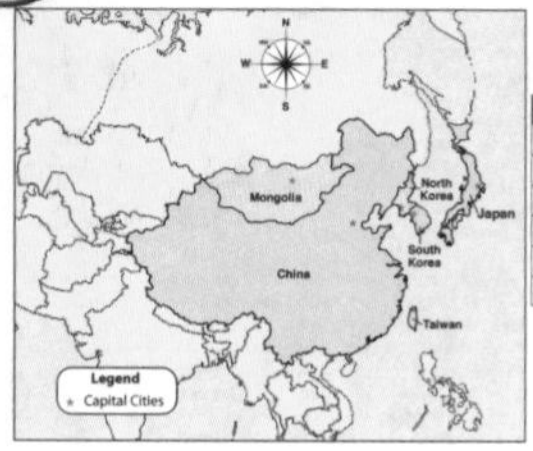

Country	Capital
China	Beijing
South Korea	Seoul
Japan	Tokyo
North Korea	Pyongyang
Taiwan	Taipei
Mongolia	Ulaanbaatar

Use the map and the chart to answer the questions.

1. Which country is north of China? Mongolia
2. What is the capital of Japan? Tokyo
3. What is the capital of Taiwan? Taipei
4. Which four countries are east of China? North Korea, South Korea, Taiwan, and Japan
5. What are the capitals of North Korea and South Korea? North Korea: Pyongyang South Korea: Seoul

92 Friday

Week 8 **Page 95**

Read It! Fiction

Read the journal entry. Then answer the questions.

Jesse's Journal

August 12

I'm so thankful we're all okay. I never imagined I'd have to go through something as terrifying as what happened yesterday. At first I thought we were about to have a regular thunderstorm. The sky got dark and the wind picked up. Dad came in early from the fields on his tractor. Then my sister Julia said, "Look at the sky. Doesn't it look weird?"

We went to the window and saw strange, heavy clouds. The sky had an eerie yellowish tint. I heard the wind begin to roar and started to feel frightened. Mom told us to run to the storm cellar, but I wanted to go to my room to get some of my things first. Mom grabbed me and made me stay with everyone else. As we ran toward the storm cellar, I saw a long, thin cloud drop down from the sky and touch the ground. The noise grew louder, like a train rushing straight at us. My little brother Mark started to cry. I picked him up and carried him down the steps into the cellar.

We turned on the emergency lamps and huddled together. Above us, we heard horrible sounds of crashing and tearing that seemed to go on forever. All I could think about was losing my computer and MP3 player. I knew Julia was worried about the clothes she had just bought, and Mark was thinking about his favorite toys.

When it finally grew quiet again, we came upstairs. The whole house was gone—just gone. The garage next to the house hadn't been touched, and the barn was fine. We all had the exact same reaction. Instead of crying about what we had lost, we hugged each other and cried because everyone was safe. We still had what mattered most—our family.

1. **When the tornado hits, what do the family's children think about most?**
   - Ⓐ the cars and farm equipment
   - ● their belongings
   - Ⓒ their home
   - Ⓓ their pets and farm animals
2. **How do you think Jesse feels about storms?**
   - Ⓐ They are part of the natural world.
   - Ⓑ They are symbols of spring and rebirth.
   - ● They remind you that life can change quickly.
   - Ⓓ They are minor annoyances that are soon forgotten.
3. **After the storm, why does the family cry?**
   - ● They are thankful to be safe.
   - Ⓑ They know they have to rebuild their house.
   - Ⓒ They are very frightened.
   - Ⓓ They are sad about losing their belongings.
4. **Which statement is a theme of the passage?**
   - Ⓐ There is no love like a mother's love.
   - ● Family is the most important thing.
   - Ⓒ Taking care of your possessions is important.
   - Ⓓ Fear can make bad events better.

Monday Week 8 95

Page 96

Write It Right

Rewrite each sentence, correcting the errors.

1. wear did you find all of them tomatos carrots and, onions.
   Where did you find all of those tomatoes, carrots, and onions?
2. before diner I always help set the tabel, afterword I help clean up
   Before dinner, I always help set the table, and afterward I help clean up.
3. I did'nt get no candie, when I went to the groshery store.
   I didn't get any candy when I went to the grocery store.
4. I no that you where going throu my stuff accused roxy.
   "I know that you were going through my stuff!" accused Roxy.

MATH TIME

Use the information on the list to answer the questions.

1. How much did Ms. Boomer spend on her Hawaiian vacation? $2,096.86
2. To pay for her vacation, Ms. Boomer saved $175.00 a month for a year. After her vacation, how much of her savings did she have left? $3.14
3. How much did Ms. Boomer spend on transportation? $945.83
4. If Ms. Boomer stayed at a hotel for four nights, what was the nightly rate for her room? $150.12

Hawaiian Vacation Expenses	
$750.83	Airfare
$600.48	Hotel
$195.00	Car rental
$39.80	Souvenirs
$150.00	Scuba diving and surfing
$320.00	Meals
$40.75	Park entrance fees

96 Monday

Page 97

SPELL IT

A **compound word** is made by joining two smaller words.

Rewrite each of this week's spelling words correctly. Then draw a line between the two words that make up each compound word.

1. laughinstock: laughing|stock
2. eyewittnes: eye|witness
3. straigtforward: straight|forward
4. grandaughter: grand|daughter
5. downstreem: down|stream
6. underpoppulated: under|populated
7. beachcomer: beach|comber
8. tundershower: thunder|shower
9. fetherwate: feather|weight
10. wheelbarow: wheel|barrow
11. hedquarters: head|quarters
12. overremphacize: over|emphasize

In My Own Words

Do you think parents should limit the amount of time that kids play video games and watch TV? Why or why not?

Sample answer:
I think that parents should limit the amount of time that kids play video games and watch TV because it's important for kids to have a variety of different activities. Playing video games and watching TV are not bad in moderation. But kids need time for homework and for doing more active things such as riding bikes or playing sports. If parents don't put limits on TV and game time, most kids will just park themselves in front of the screen and not get up!

Tuesday Week 8 97

Page 98

LANGUAGE LINES

A **subject** and a **verb** must agree in number.

Circle the correct form of the verb. Write whether the subject is *singular* or *plural* on the line.

1. Cat shows are large events that **attracts** (**attract**) many pet owners. plural
2. I **enters** (**enter**) my cat in the house-pet category. singular
3. Special breeds **competes** (**compete**) in a different category. plural
4. A judge gently (**examines**) **examine** a cat's bushy tail. singular
5. My cat (**yawns**) **yawn** as she waits her turn. singular
6. The other cats **prances** (**prance**) around the ring. plural

MATH TIME

Meredith and Derek were playing the probability game with marbles. Derek put 2 pink marbles, 6 blue marbles, and 16 green marbles in a bag. What is the probability of Meredith randomly selecting a marble that is...?

1. pink 1 in 12
2. blue 1 in 4
3. green 2 in 3
4. pink or blue 1 in 3
5. pink or green 3 in 4
6. blue or green 11 in 12

98 Tuesday

Page 99

Read It! Nonfiction

Read the passage and map. Then answer the questions.

Mesoamerica Before the Spanish

Long before the Spanish invaded Central America, a number of civilizations existed in the area now known as Mesoamerica. The map and timeline below provide dates and locations of a few of these extraordinary cultures.

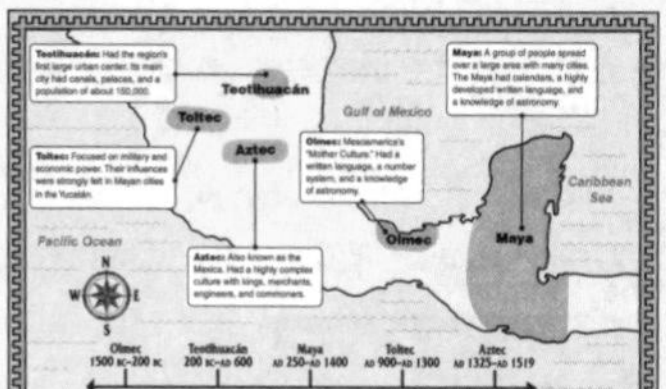

1. **Which two cultures did *not* exist around the same time?**
   - Ⓐ the Teotihuacán and the Maya
   - ● the Toltec and the Olmec
   - Ⓒ the Toltec and the Maya
   - Ⓓ the Aztec and the Maya
2. **According to the information on the map, which two cultures are known for their use of written language?**
   - Ⓐ the Aztec and the Maya
   - ● the Olmec and the Maya
   - Ⓒ the Toltec and the Olmec
   - Ⓓ the Teotihuacán and the Aztec
3. **Which culture extended the farthest south?**
   - ● the Maya
   - Ⓑ the Olmec
   - Ⓒ the Teotihuacán
   - Ⓓ the Aztec
4. **What information can be found on the map?**
   - Ⓐ the boundaries of modern-day Mexico
   - Ⓑ where the Spanish landed in 1519
   - ● where each pre-1519 culture was located
   - Ⓓ which countries the Spanish conquered

Wednesday Week 8 99

Page 100

Vo·cab·u·lar·y

Fill in the blanks with the correct idioms.

fork over	wash his hands of	hook, line, and sinker
tightfisted	shooting the breeze	paying through the nose
way off base	gave him the lowdown	feeling like a million bucks

Pablo and Jake were just hanging out, shooting the breeze like on any other day, when Jake mentioned he'd heard about an amazing deal on the Internet. For thirty bucks, Jake claimed, anyone could be a game-tester and get free video games. Now, Pablo had just spent $60 on his last game, and he was tired of paying through the nose every time a new game came out, so this idea was very attractive.

Pablo knew Jake was pretty stingy and tightfisted. The guy wouldn't even fork over a couple of bucks for ice cream without comparing prices to see if he could get a better deal elsewhere. He was smart with his money, so Pablo believed that this deal had to be a sure thing.

Jake helped Pablo register online and gave him the lowdown on how the program worked. Within hours, Pablo had received a gazillion e-mails trying to sell him a gazillion things, but no games to test, and nothing free.

"Huh!" said Jake. "I guess I was way off base on this one."

As it turned out, the whole thing was a scam, and the boys had fallen for it hook, line, and sinker.

Fortunately, Pablo was able to change his e-mail address and wash his hands of the entire mess. But he was still out $30. And instead of happily playing free video games and feeling like a million bucks, he simply felt like an idiot.

100 Wednesday

Page 101

LANGUAGE LINES

Some nouns have unusual, or **irregular**, plural forms.

Write the plural form of each noun. Use a dictionary to help you, if necessary.

1. deer deer
2. leaf leaves
3. hoof hooves
4. woman women
5. louse lice
6. alumnus alumni
7. moose moose
8. crisis crises
9. criterion criteria
10. person people
11. loaf loaves
12. cactus cacti or cactuses
13. shelf shelves
14. ox oxen
15. sheep sheep

In My Own Words

What do you think are the five most important jobs in the world? Why are each of these jobs so important?

Sample answer:
The five most important jobs are:
1. President of the United States, because not only is he (or she) in charge of domestic affairs, but the president also has a heavy influence on countries around the world
2. emergency room doctors, because they often have to make quick decisions under pressure to save peoples' lives
3. army generals, because their strategies often determine whether or not a country wins a war
4. parents, because they are responsible for their children's safety, health, and happiness
5. teachers, because they have a huge influence on young people's minds and give them important knowledge

Thursday Week 8 101

Page 102

Mind Jigglers

From Here to There

Write the names of the towns you would visit on each route to Grandma's house. Then write the total number of miles you would travel.

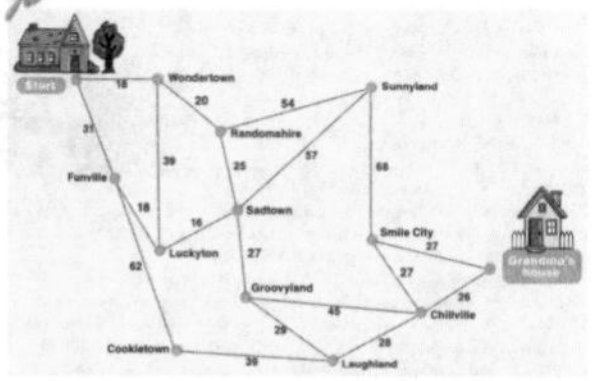

1. If you wanted to get there in the fewest miles possible, you would go through... Wondertown, Randomshire, Sadtown, Groovyland, Chillville Total miles: 161
2. If you were on a bike and couldn't travel more than 30 miles each day, you would go through... Wondertown, Randomshire, Sadtown, Groovyland, Laughland, Chillville Total miles: 173
3. If you wanted to visit Groovyland but avoid Sadtown on the way, you would go through... Funville, Cookietown, Laughland, Groovyland, Chillville Total miles: 232
4. If you wanted to visit 11 towns before you got to Grandma's house, but you did not want to visit any town more than once, you would go through... Funville, Cookietown, Laughland, Groovyland, Sadtown, Luckyton, Wondertown, Randomshire, Sunnyland, Smile City, Chillville Total miles: 438

102 Thursday

MATH TIME

Exponents

The large number is called a *base*.
The small number is called an *exponent*.
It shows how many times the base is used as a factor.

5^2 is read as "five squared."
It tells you to multiply 5 by itself two times.
$5 \times 5 = 25$

4^3 is read as "four cubed."
It tells you to multiply 4 by itself three times.
$4 \times 4 \times 4 = 64$

2^5 is read as "two to the fifth power."
It tells you to multiply 2 by itself five times.
$2 \times 2 \times 2 \times 2 \times 2 = 32$

A. Solve these problems using exponents.

1. 4^2 = **16**
2. 2^3 = **8**
3. 3^5 = **243**
4. 8^2 = **64**
5. 4^5 = **1,024**
6. 5^3 = **125**
7. 2^4 = **16**
8. 6^3 = **216**

B. Solve these equations using exponents.

1. $2^3 + 3^3$ = **31**
2. $6^2 + 4^3$ = **100**
3. $6^3 - 4^2$ = **200**
4. $3^2 - 2^3$ = **1**
5. $5^3 \times 3^3$ = **675**
6. $3^2 \times 3^3$ = **243**
7. $3^3 + 3^3$ = **3**
8. $5^2 + 5^2$ = **25**

Friday WEEK 8 103

Geography

Countries of South America

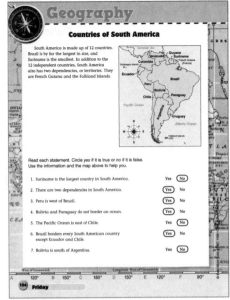

South America is made up of 12 countries. Brazil is by far the largest in size, and Suriname is the smallest. In addition to the 12 independent countries, South America also has two dependencies, or territories. They are French Guiana and the Falkland Islands.

Read each statement. Circle *yes* if it is true or *no* if it is false.
Use the information and the map above to help you.

1. Suriname is the largest country in South America. — Yes (No)
2. There are two dependencies in South America. — (Yes) No
3. Peru is west of Brazil. — (Yes) No
4. Bolivia and Paraguay do not border an ocean. — (Yes) No
5. The Pacific Ocean is east of Chile. — Yes (No)
6. Brazil borders every South American country except Ecuador and Chile. — (Yes) No
7. Bolivia is south of Argentina. — Yes (No)

104 Friday

Read It! Fiction

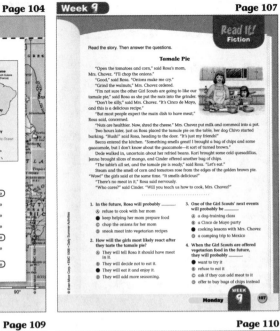

Read the story. Then answer the questions.

Tamale Pie

"Open the tomatoes and corn," said Rosa's mom, Mrs. Chavez. "I'll chop the onions."
"Good," said Rosa. "Onions make me cry."
"Grind the walnuts," Mrs. Chavez ordered.
"I'm not sure the Girl Scouts are going to like our tamale pie," said Rosa as she put the nuts into the grinder.
"Don't be silly," said Mrs. Chavez. "It's Cinco de Mayo, and this is a delicious recipe."
"But most people expect the main dish to have meat," Rosa said, concerned.
"Nuts are healthier. Now, shred the cheese." Mrs. Chavez put milk and cornmeal into a pot.
Two hours later, just as Rosa placed the tamale pie on the table, her dog Chivo started barking. "Hush!" said Rosa, heading to the door. "It's just my friends!"
Becca entered the kitchen. "Something smells great! I brought a bag of chips and some guacamole, but I don't know about the guacamole—it sort of turned brown."
Dede walked in, uncertain about her refried beans. Kari brought some cold quesadillas, Jenna brought slices of mango, and Cinder offered another bag of chips.
"The table's all set, and the tamale pie is ready," said Rosa. "Let's eat."
Steam and the smell of corn and tomatoes rose from the edges of the golden brown pie. "Wow!" the girls said at the same time. "It smells delicious!"
"There's no meat in it," Rosa said nervously.
"Who cares?" said Cinder. "Will you teach us how to cook, Mrs. Chavez?"

1. In the future, Rosa will probably _____
   Ⓐ refuse to cook with her mom
   ● keep helping her mom prepare food
   Ⓒ chop the onions for her mom
   Ⓓ sneak meat into vegetarian recipes

2. How will the girls most likely react after they taste the tamale pie?
   Ⓐ They will tell Rosa it should have meat
   Ⓑ They will decide not to eat it
   ● They will eat it and enjoy it
   Ⓓ They will add more seasoning

3. One of the Girl Scouts' next events will probably be _____
   Ⓐ a dog-training class
   Ⓑ a Cinco de Mayo party
   ● cooking lessons with Mrs. Chavez
   Ⓓ a camping trip to Mexico

4. When the Girl Scouts are offered vegetarian food in the future, they will probably _____
   ● want to try it
   Ⓑ refuse to eat it
   Ⓒ ask if they can add meat to it
   Ⓓ offer to buy bags of chips instead

Monday WEEK 9 107

Write It Right

Rewrite each sentence, correcting the errors.

1. I think we should use the red white and blew rapping paper?
   I think we should use the red, white, and blue wrapping paper.

2. My Aunt took a towel sum sun scream, a book and a apple to the beech
   My aunt took a towel, some sunscreen, a book, and an apple to the beach.

3. Even thou John raysed his hand politely the teacher did'nt call on him
   Even though John raised his hand politely, the teacher didn't call on him.

4. Dad can you pickup Carolyn and I from skool tommorrow.
   Dad, can you pick up Carolyn and me from school tomorrow?

MATH TIME

Use <, >, or = to make each math sentence true.

1. $\frac{2}{3}$ **>** $\frac{1}{5}$
2. $\frac{2}{3}$ **=** $\frac{4}{6}$
3. $1\frac{1}{2}$ **>** $\frac{3}{4}$
4. $3\frac{1}{4}$ **<** $\frac{19}{5}$
5. $\frac{4}{5}$ **<** $\frac{8}{9}$
6. $\frac{6}{10}$ **>** $\frac{1}{4}$
7. $4\frac{2}{3}$ **=** $\frac{14}{3}$
8. $\frac{2}{3}$ **>** $\frac{2}{5}$
9. $\frac{1}{2}$ **=** $\frac{2}{3} \times \frac{3}{4}$
10. $\frac{2}{3} \times \frac{1}{2}$ **<** $\frac{2}{4} \times \frac{3}{5}$

106 Monday

SPELL IT

The suffixes *–able* and *–ible* form adjectives that mean "likely to," "can be," or "worthy of."

Fill in the correct suffix, either *–ible* or *–able*, to complete the spelling words for the week.

1. access **ible**
2. convert **ible**
3. maneuver **able**
4. respons **ible**
5. adjust **able**
6. invinc **ible**
7. negoti **able**
8. believ **able**
9. elig **ible**
10. inconsol **able**
11. exchange **able**
12. compat **ible**

In My Own Words

If you could make up one law that everyone in the world must follow, what law would it be? Why?

Sample answer:
My law would be to shorten the school week. I think students would be happier if they had more time to relax and be with their families and friends. If we had just four days of school a week, then we'd have three whole days for fun and other important activities, such as sports or music. I think kids would be more well-rested and ready for school after a three-day weekend!

Tuesday WEEK 9 109

LANGUAGE LINES

Quotation marks are used to show dialogue, or what someone has said.

Rewrite these sentences to correctly punctuate the dialogue. The first one has been done for you.

1. How are we going to get all these dishes washed Martina wondered?
   "How are we going to get all these dishes washed?" Martina wondered.

2. Lou called out I'll be waiting for you at the bus stop tomorrow!
   Lou called out, "I'll be waiting for you at the bus stop tomorrow!"

3. No. Barbara repeated I don't know where the hammer is
   "No," Barbara repeated. "I don't know where the hammer is."

4. I want to take an X-ray of your arm. the doctor told his patient.
   "I want to take an X-ray of your arm," the doctor told his patient.

5. Do you want to try to solve these equations together Mary asked?
   "Do you want to try to solve these equations together?" Mary asked.

MATH TIME

Solve each word problem.

1. Tim ran 100 yards in 21 seconds, and Juan ran 100 feet in 8 seconds. Who was running faster and why?
   Tim was running faster, because if Juan had run at Tim's pace, it would have taken him 24 seconds to finish.

2. Frances walked 10 meters while Darcy walked 1,200 centimeters. Who walked farther? Why?
   Darcy walked farther, because 1,200 centimeters equals 12 meters.

110 Tuesday

Read It! Nonfiction

Read the article. Then answer the questions.

The Man Who Loved the Sea

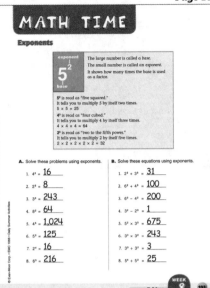

Jacques Cousteau was born in France in 1910. Although he was sickly as a child, he learned to swim at an early age and developed a love for the ocean. He joined the French navy in 1933, and it was there that he first used a pair of underwater goggles. Amazed at what he saw beneath the sea, he decided to build a device that would allow people to breathe underwater. In 1942, he finished the Aqua-Lung, a piece of early underwater breathing equipment that would eventually lead to the SCUBA diving gear used today.

After World War II, Cousteau began his life's work onboard the research ship *Calypso*. He worked with divers and scientists to photograph and gather samples of underwater plants and animals. In doing so, he learned about many ocean creatures that had never been studied before.

In 1960, he successfully worked to stop nuclear waste from being dumped into the Mediterranean Sea. He worked tirelessly to improve the ecological conditions of the world's oceans and won many awards for his efforts. His television show, *The Undersea World of Jacques Cousteau*, ran from 1968 to 1976. The series helped raise awareness of the creatures who inhabit the world's oceans. Cousteau died in 1997 at the age of 87 and is still celebrated as one of the most important explorers and environmentalists of the twentieth century.

1. Which of these happened before Jacques Cousteau joined the navy?
   Ⓐ He worked on the *Calypso*.
   ● He learned to swim.
   Ⓒ He had a television series.
   Ⓓ He won many awards.

2. After World War II, what did Cousteau do?
   Ⓐ He began using underwater goggles.
   Ⓑ He became very ill.
   ● He worked on the *Calypso*.
   Ⓓ He joined the navy.

3. Cousteau developed the Aqua-Lung _____
   ● after joining the navy
   Ⓑ while working on the *Calypso*
   Ⓒ after winning awards
   Ⓓ before learning to swim

4. Which of these events happened last?
   Ⓐ Cousteau built an underwater breathing device.
   Ⓑ Cousteau protested against dumping nuclear waste.
   Ⓒ Cousteau joined the French navy.
   ● Cousteau's TV show raised awareness of the world's oceans.

Wednesday WEEK 9 111

Vo·cab·u·lar·y

A **base word** is a word that can stand alone before prefixes, suffixes, or other word parts are added.

keep**ing** **un**happy
careful **pre**view

A. Write the base word of each word below. Watch out for spelling changes.

1. unbelievable — **believe**
2. forgetful — **forget**
3. dismissed — **miss**
4. uncertainty — **certain**
5. beautiful — **beauty**
6. timidity — **timid**
7. carelessly — **care**
8. nonsensical — **sense**

B. Complete each sentence by writing a base word from Activity A on the line.

1. Do not **forget** to return your library book.
2. Tim felt nervous and **timid** about giving his class presentation.
3. If you don't hurry, you will **miss** your next class.
4. Iris wrapped the fragile teacup in tissue paper with **care**.
5. We admired the forest for its natural **beauty**.
6. Cheryl was absolutely **certain** that she had won first place.
7. You would not **believe** the news I just heard about the game!
8. Marcia's cat could **sense** that the neighbor's dog was nearby.

112 Wednesday

LANGUAGE LINES

Parts of speech include nouns, pronouns, prepositions, adjectives, verbs, adverbs, and clauses.

Write the letter of the part of speech that matches the underlined word or words.

d 1. My family <u>traveled</u> to France last summer.
h 2. Adam was <u>very</u> pleased with his performance.
e 3. We brought <u>our</u> books to class.
f 4. Shelly <u>can</u> walk to the store from her house.
g 5. <u>I have a puppy</u> that I play with every day.
b 6. The fans inside the gym were cheering loudly.
a 7. <u>She</u> made the winning goal for her team.
c 8. Australia is the <u>smallest</u> continent.

a. personal pronoun
b. prepositional phrase
c. adjective
d. past tense verb
e. possessive pronoun
f. helping verb
g. independent clause
h. adverb

In My Own Words

What is the best gift that you have ever given someone? What made it so special?

Sample answer:
The best gift I have ever given was a memory book for my parents' wedding anniversary. I collected old photos of the two of them together through the years and put them in a special scrapbook that my parents can keep adding to. They loved it because it had personal meaning to them, and it was a record of everything they had done together over the years.

Thursday WEEK 9 113

Page 114

Mind Jigglers

Say Cheese!

A. People say "cheese" when they have their photos taken because the **/ee/** sound makes their mouths widen into a smile. What are three other food words that would also do this?

Sample answers: 1. beans 2. peas 3. cream

B. Use the clues to figure out the words. The letters in each word can all be found in the word *CAMERA*.

- a male sheep: ram
- the card before 2: ace
- a speed contest: race
- a female horse: mare
- rich milk to whip: cream
- means *arrived*: came
- to fill by force: cram

C. Carrie has arranged her photos in a display of 9 rows. The first row has 7 photos, the second has 6, the third has 7, the fourth has 6, and so on. How many photos are in Carrie's display?

59 photos

Carrie is in every fourth photo. How many photos is Carrie in?

14 photos

D. Michael traveled to Yellowstone National Park with his family. He had a camera, but he did not take any pictures. Give three possible reasons. Sample answers:

1. His battery died.
2. His memory card was full.
3. He was enjoying himself so much that he forgot to take pictures.

E. Write a four-word sentence about taking a picture, usir Sample answer:

I photographed our family.

Page 115

MATH TIME

Riddle Me This

A. Study the table below to see which sports students like to watch on TV.

	Football	Basketball	Soccer	Baseball
Boys	10	4	11	3
Girls	5	9	12	1

Now use the information to draw a double bar graph below. Match the colors in the table to the colors on your graph.

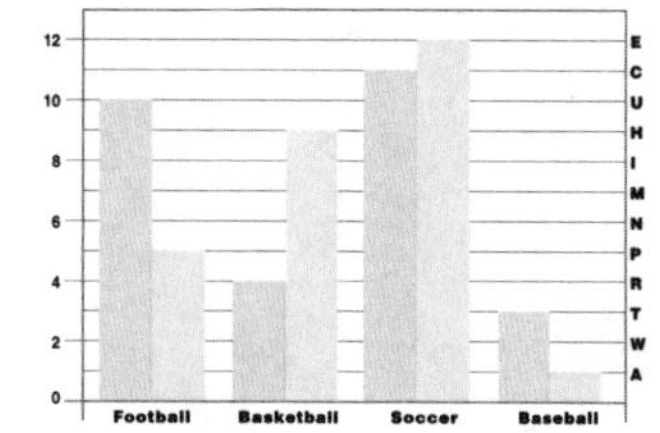

12
10
8
6
4
2
0
Football
Basketball
Soccer
Baseball
E
C
U
H
I
M
N
P
R
T
W
A

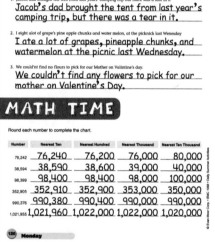

B. Each line below has a sport and a gender listed under it corresponding to one of the bars you drew on the graph. Look for the letter along the right that aligns with the top of each bar. Write that letter on the corresponding line to spell out the answer to this riddle:

What is bought by the yard and worn by the foot?

C	A	R	P	E	T
soccer boys	basketball girls	basketball boys	football girls	soccer girls	baseball boys

Page 116

Geography

Northern Europe

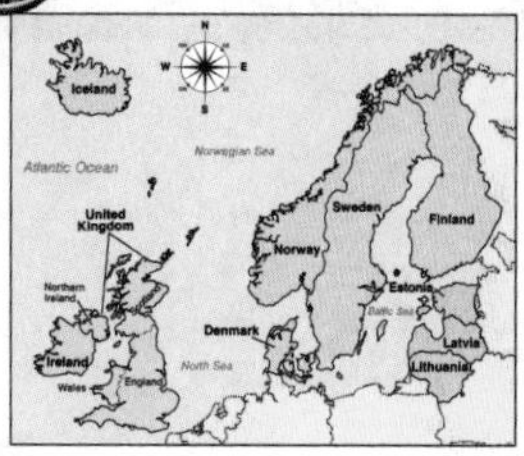

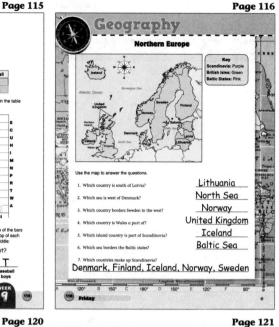

Key
Scandinavia: Purple
British Isles: Green
Baltic States: Pink
Iceland
Atlantic Ocean
Norwegian Sea
United Kingdom
Northern Ireland
Ireland
Wales
England
Norway
Sweden
Finland
Estonia
Latvia
Lithuania
Denmark
North Sea

Use the map to answer the questions.

1. Which country is south of Latvia? Lithuania
2. Which sea is west of Denmark? North Sea
3. Which country borders Sweden to the west? Norway
4. Which country is Wales a part of? United Kingdom
5. Which island country is part of Scandinavia? Iceland
6. Which sea borders the Baltic states? Baltic Sea
7. Which countries make up Scandinavia? Denmark, Finland, Iceland, Norway, Sweden

Page 119

Read It! Fiction

Read the story. Then answer the questions.

Three Parts for Three Characters

Denzel could hear the sounds of the song "Follow the Yellow Brick Road" as he walked closer to the auditorium. He was relieved that the auditions weren't over. He really wanted to try out for the sixth-grade production of *The Wizard of Oz*. Waiting in the hall were his two best friends, Colin and Felipe. Colin was walking on his hands in a wide circle. Then he did a cartwheel into a back handspring, finishing with a back flip. Felipe was doing his favorite herky-jerky robot dance.

Just as Denzel reached the boys, there was a sudden boom outside. "What was that?" Denzel shouted. He had a voice that could be loud and strong one moment and drop to a whisper the next instant.

"It's thunder," Colin laughed. "You should audition for the role of the character who needs courage!"

"Come on!" Felipe urged with a stiff bow to end his dance. "We'll miss our turns!"

The trio hurried inside the auditorium. A girl named Rachel, with hair teased like a lion's mane, was beginning her audition. The boys watched her. She pranced around the stage like a lion, but she spoke very quietly, and it was hard to hear her. When she finished, Felipe auditioned by dancing like a robot. Colin went next, showing his acrobatic skills. Denzel went last.

When the auditions ended, each boy had the perfect part for his talents. Colin was the Scarecrow, who is supposed to flop, slip, and slide all over the stage. Felipe's robot moves were just like the Tin Man in his rusty metal suit. And Denzel's booming roar and soft whisper made him the best Cowardly Lion the play could have.

1. **There is evidence in the passage to support the idea that Denzel ______.**
   - Ⓐ has never acted in a play before
   - Ⓑ is always late
   - ● is easily startled
   - Ⓓ does not get along with Colin
2. **What is the reason that Denzel got the part of the Cowardly Lion?**
   - Ⓐ It was the only part available.
   - Ⓑ He was scared of the thunder.
   - Ⓒ No one else auditioned for the part.
   - ● He had the right voice for the role.
3. **Why did Colin get the role of Scarecrow?**
   - ● He is good at doing acrobatics.
   - Ⓑ He is a very serious person.
   - Ⓒ He used dance moves during the audition.
   - Ⓓ He had his hair teased for the part.
4. **In the passage, which of these happens first?**
   - Ⓐ The boys get the perfect parts.
   - ● Colin and Felipe practice in the hallway.
   - Ⓒ Denzel hears a loud clap of thunder.
   - Ⓓ A girl named Rachel finishes her audition.

Page 120

Write It Right

Rewrite each sentence, correcting the errors.

1. Jacobs dad braught the tent from last years' camping trip but there was a tare in it
   Jacob's dad brought the tent from last year's camping trip, but there was a tear in it.
2. I eight alot of grape's pine apple chunks and water melon, at the picknick last Wenesday
   I ate a lot of grapes, pineapple chunks, and watermelon at the picnic last Wednesday.
3. We could'nt find no flours to pick for our Mother on Valintine's day.
   We couldn't find any flowers to pick for our mother on Valentine's Day.

MATH TIME

Round each number to complete the chart.

Number	Nearest Ten	Nearest Hundred	Nearest Thousand	Nearest Ten Thousand
76,242	76,240	76,200	76,000	80,000
38,594	38,590	38,600	39,000	40,000
98,399	98,400	98,400	98,000	100,000
352,905	352,910	352,900	353,000	350,000
990,376	990,380	990,400	990,000	990,000
1,021,955	1,021,960	1,022,000	1,022,000	1,020,000

Page 121

SPELL IT

When c comes before e, i, or y, it makes the soft /s/ sound.
When g comes before e, i, or y, it makes the soft /j/ sound.

Fill in the missing letter or letters to make the spelling words for the week. Then circle the letter or letters that make the **/s/** or **/j/** sound.

1. a gen cy
2. cy clone
3. emer gency
4. sur gi cal
5. conta gious
6. myth olo gy
7. rhi noce os
8. inno cence
9. ci na mon
10. pre cise
11. gen e tic
12. gymna sium

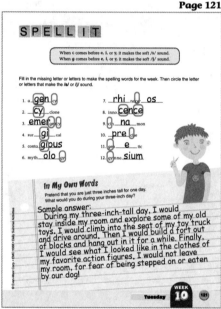

In My Own Words

Pretend that you are just three inches tall for one day. What would you do during your three-inch day?

Sample answer:
During my three-inch-tall day, I would stay inside my room and explore some of my old toys. I would climb into the seat of my toy truck and drive around. Then I would build a fort out of blocks and hang out in it for a while. Finally, I would see what I looked like in the clothes of my favorite action figures. I would not leave my room, for fear of being stepped on or eaten by our dog!

Page 122

LANGUAGE LINES

The **antecedent** of a pronoun is the noun (or nouns) to which it refers.

The antecedent does not have to be in the same sentence as the pronoun.

The rider rode to the next station. There, a fresh horse was waiting for him.
(antecedent) (pronoun)

Circle each pronoun. Then draw an arrow from the pronoun to its antecedent.

1. The Pony Express helped unify a nation. It was very successful.
2. About 180 riders took part. They were on the trail day and night.
3. The riders traveled in any weather, no matter how bad it got.
4. Mail was delivered in 10 days during the summer months. It took two weeks in the winter.
5. Many people depended on the Pony Express, and they were thankful for its services.
6. A rider for the Pony Express had to be an expert. He also had to be willing to risk death.

MATH TIME

Solve the word problems.

Skyler took a lot of photos on his Grand Canyon trip. He deleted one-third of them. Then he uploaded half of the remaining photos to a photo-managing site. He ordered prints of one-fourth of the uploaded photos and gave half of the prints away. The number of prints he gave away was 24. How many photos did Skyler originally take?

576 photos

Skyler's little sister Jasmine took a lot of photos, too. She took 354 photos altogether: 286 were of scenery, and 128 were of people. How many were of both scenery and people?

60 photos

Jasmine put 25% of the photos of people in an album. How many photos did she put in the album?

32 photos

Page 123

Read It! Nonfiction

Read the article. Then answer the questions.

The World in a Pond

An ecosystem is a community of living and nonliving things that work together. Organisms, light, heat, soil, water, and the atmosphere are all parts of an ecosystem. Any alteration to an ecosystem—such as changes in temperature, the kinds of animals living there, or pollution—can affect all parts of it. This can be especially obvious in the small, enclosed ecosystem of a pond.

In a pond, sunlight helps tiny plants called *algae* grow. Algae release oxygen, which fish need in order to breathe. Algae are also food for other tiny organisms, which are in turn eaten by fish. The fish then give off carbon dioxide, which plants use to grow.

Imagine what would happen, however, if certain conditions changed in the pond. For example, if sunlight didn't reach the pond because of thick pollution, or if the temperature of the water grew colder or warmer, the algae wouldn't grow. Without algae, there would first be less oxygen. Tiny organisms would starve. Fish would die from the lack of oxygen. Plants would then die without the carbon dioxide that fish give off. And larger animals that eat the plants and smaller animals would not get enough food. Even humans, who eat the plants, fish, and larger animals, would feel the impact. The whole ecosystem would suffer.

1. **Which of these would happen first if algae stopped growing in a pond?**
   - Ⓐ Fish would die.
   - Ⓑ There would be less carbon dioxide.
   - ● There would be less oxygen.
   - Ⓓ Plants would die.
2. **After the tiny organisms that eat algae died, the next thing to happen would be that ______.**
   - ● the fish would die
   - Ⓑ plants would lack carbon dioxide
   - Ⓒ humans would go hungry
   - Ⓓ larger animals would have less food
3. **Plants would die in a pond after ______.**
   - Ⓐ the amount of oxygen decreased
   - Ⓑ humans were affected
   - Ⓒ larger animals went hungry
   - ● the amount of carbon dioxide decreased
4. **Which of these would be the last to feel the effects of a lack of algae?**
   - Ⓐ fish
   - Ⓑ plants
   - ● humans
   - Ⓓ tiny organisms

Page 124

Vo·cab·u·lar·y

Homographs are words that are spelled the same but have different meanings. They can also be different parts of speech.

Identify the part of speech for the bold word in each sentence and write it on the fist line. Then, on the second line, write another sentence using the *homograph* of the bold word. Use the definitions in the box to help you.

- **sage** *n.* an herb; *adj.* wise
- **flounder** *n.* a marine flatfish; *v.* to struggle clumsily
- **loom** *n.* a frame for weaving; *v.* to appear in front of, looking big or scary
- **spell** *n.* a magical charm; *v.* to give the letters of a word in order
- **reel** *n.* a device for winding string; *v.* to stagger or whirl

Sample sentences:

1. Report cards **loom** on the schedule just before winter break. verb
   Sarah weaved a new blanket on her loom.
2. After fishing all day, we had **flounder** for dinner. noun
   Brad began to flounder awkwardly on the dance floor.
3. The guidance counselor offered **sage** advice on applying to colleges. adjective
   Mom added some sage to the stuffing.
4. I wish I knew a **spell** for growing tall. noun
   Erica needs to spell a difficult word to win the spelling bee.
5. An hour of math homework is enough to make my brain **reel**. verb
   My grandparents showed me an old film reel of their wedding.

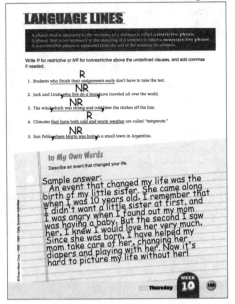

LANGUAGE LINES

A phrase that is necessary to the meaning of a sentence is called a **restrictive phrase**. A phrase that is not necessary to the meaning of a sentence is called a **nonrestrictive phrase**. A nonrestrictive phrase is separated from the rest of the sentence by commas.

Write *R* for restrictive or *NR* for nonrestrictive above the underlined clauses, and add commas if needed.

1. Students who finish their assignments early don't have to take the test. — **R**
2. Jack and Linda who live on a boat have traveled all over the world. — **NR**
3. The wind which was strong and cold blew the clothes off the line. — **NR**
4. Climates that have both cold and warm weather are called "temperate." — **R**
5. San Pablo where Marta was born is a small town in Argentina. — **NR**

In My Own Words

Describe an event that changed your life.

Sample answer:
An event that changed my life was the birth of my little sister. She came along when I was 10 years old. I remember that I didn't want a little sister at first, and I was angry when I found out my mom was having a baby. But the second I saw her, I knew I would love her very much. Since she was born, I have helped my mom take care of her, changing her diapers and playing with her. Now it's hard to picture my life without her!

Thursday **10** (125)

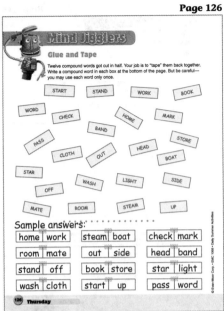

Mind Jigglers

Glue and Tape

Twelve compound words got cut in half. Your job is to "tape" them back together. Write a compound word in each box at the bottom of the page. But be careful— you may use each word only once.

START STAND WORK BOOK
WORD CHECK HOME MARK
PASS BAND STORE
CLOTH OUT HEAD BOAT
STAR WASH LIGHT SIDE
OFF MATE ROOM STEAM UP

Sample answers:

home	work	steam	boat	check	mark
room	mate	out	side	head	band
stand	off	book	store	star	light
wash	cloth	start	up	pass	word

(126) Thursday

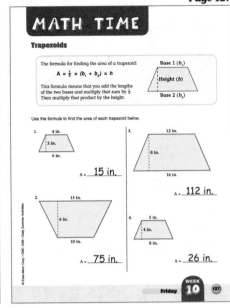

MATH TIME

Trapezoids

The formula for finding the area of a trapezoid:

$$A = \tfrac{1}{2} \times (b_1 + b_2) \times h$$

This formula means that you add the lengths of the two bases and multiply that sum by $\tfrac{1}{2}$. Then multiply that product by the height.

Base 1 (b_1)
Height (h)
Base 2 (b_2)

Use the formula to find the area of each trapezoid below.

1. 4 in. / 3 in. / 6 in. A = **15 in.**

3. 12 in. / 8 in. / 16 in. A = **112 in.**

2. 15 in. / 6 in. / 10 in. A = **75 in.**

4. 5 in. / 4 in. / 8 in. A = **26 in.**

Friday **10** (127)

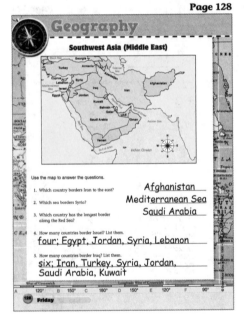

Geography

Southwest Asia (Middle East)

Use the map to answer the questions.

1. Which country borders Iran to the east?
   Afghanistan

2. Which sea borders Syria?
   Mediterranean Sea

3. Which country has the longest border along the Red Sea?
   Saudi Arabia

4. How many countries border Israel? List them.
   four; Egypt, Jordan, Syria, Lebanon

5. How many countries border Iraq? List them.
   six; Iran, Turkey, Syria, Jordan, Saudi Arabia, Kuwait

(128) Friday

summer journal